knitting on the edge

ribs . ruffles . lace . fringes . flora . points & picots

knitting on the edge

ribs • ruffles • lace • fringes • flora • points & picots

the essential collection of 350 decorative borders

nicky epstein

sixth&spring books

To my husband Howard
and "the babies": Scott, Jeff and Ken.

sixth&spring
books

Editorial Director
TRISHA MALCOLM

Art Director
CHI LING MOY

Executive Editor
CARLA SCOTT

Instructions Editor
CHARLOTTE PARRY

Instructions Proofreader
NANCY HENDERSON

Yarn Editor
VERONICA MANNO

Book Manager
MICHELLE LO

Production Manager
DAVID JOINNIDES

Photography
JACK DEUTSCH STUDIOS

President, Sixth&Spring Books
ART JOINNIDES

Library of Congress Cataloging-in-Publication Data

Epstein, Nicky

Knitting on the edge : ribs, ruffles, lace, fringes, flora, points & picots / Nicky Epstein.

p.cm.

ISBN 1-931543-40-2

1. Knitting—Patterns. 2. Borders, Ornamental (Decorative arts) I. Title.

TT825/E6422 2003

746.43'2041—dc21   2003057293

1 3 5 7 9 10 8 6 4 2

First Edition

contents

introduction

Knitting on the Edge is the book I have always wanted to write, even before I became a designer. As a knitter, I was always fascinated with edgings and borders and the beautiful enhancement that they give to every knitted piece. I think of them as a lovely extension and crowning touch to a knitted design—the icing on the cake, the extra dimension that lends distinction, the *pièce de résistance* that can turn your work into a "show-stopper."

With the infinite number of edgings available, it has always been a challenge to track them down without having to go to dozens of sources. In this book, I've attempted to consolidate them for one-stop shopping. It's a collection of edgings that I have compiled over the years from many resources, some that I have created myself, and a number of traditional ones that I have given a new twist to (pun intended).

I've included a variety of edgings from around the world, along with instructions and various techniques showing how to create and incorporate them into your knitted piece most effectively. You'll find everything from ribs to ruffles, fringes to lace, points to picots.

Each chapter features an original design incorporating one of my favorite edgings. The simplicity of the designs will allow you to interchange a border of your choice. I hope these edgings will contribute to the pleasure of all knitters and designers and encourage them to take their knitted pieces to new creative heights.

Completing this book has been a long journey for me, but I feel a great satisfaction in having created a single source book of edgings, one that I've been searching for…for years!

Happy knitting,

Nicky Epstein

t e x t u r e

In order to illustrate the effect of texture, the following swatches show the same leaf edging, knit with a variety of yarns to create totally different looks. Yarn with a smooth finish and tight twist will produce a much crisper effect whereas plush textures such as angora or mohair create a soft focus that has a gentle appeal. Don't shy away from novelty yarns—with these, you can knit the most creative borders of all.

1	bouclé	7	bulky wool
2	linen	8	silk
3	angora	9	silk wool
4	chenille	10	mohair
5	eyelash	11	cashmere
6	ribbon	12	alpaca

8

7

10

8

9

11

12

9

13

size

With the wide variety of yarns available, it's important to carefully consider yarn size when knitting. On these swatches, I used needles ranging from size #2 to #15 and corresponding yarn. An edging or border takes on an altogether different personality when the scale is varied from very fine to extra chunky. Traditional edgings will adopt a much more contemporary look when worked with bulky yarns.

13 thick and thin
14 baby fine wool
15 cotton

14

15

notes

on using this book

Directional Symbols

There are several ways to create edgings: knitting from the bottom up, knitting from the top down, or knitting separately, then turning the edging horizontally in order to pick up stitches along the selvage edge or sewing onto the main piece. In the instructions, we have used the symbols shown below to indicate the direction in which the edging was knit. In many cases, the edgings in this book are reversible.

▲ Knit from bottom up: Cast-on edge is the lower edge.

▼ Knit from the top down: Bound-off edge is the lower edge.

▶ Knit separately: Stitches can be picked up or sewn on.

◄► Reversible: Both sides are the same or equally attractive.

Standard Yarn Weights

In the "Patterns" chapter, next to the suggested yarn in the Materials section, we have used the Standard Yarn Weight System for ease in substitution. If you plan to substitute a yarn, be sure to knit a gauge swatch and check that it matches the original gauge in the pattern and has a similar appearance to the original yarn used in the pattern. These standard yarn weights can be used for any pattern.

Making Bobbles

There are many different ways to make bobbles. We've included instructions for the two most basic ones on page 164 for you to use as desired. Some variations to these basic bobbles have been written out at the beginning of the edging instruction.

For stitches and abbreviations used in this book, see pages 164 and 165.

Standard Yarn Weight System

Categories of yarn, gauge ranges, and recommended needle sizes

Yarn Weight Symbol & Category Names	1 Super Fine	2 Fine	3 Light	4 Medium	5 Bulky	6 Super Bulky
Knit Gauge Range* in Stockinette Stitch to 4 inches	27–32 sts	23–26 sts	21–24 sts	16–20 sts	12–15 sts	6–11 sts
Recommended Needle in Metric Size Range	2.25–3.25 mm	3.25–3.75 mm	3.75–4.5 mm	4.5–5.5 mm	5.5–8 mm	8 mm and larger
Recommended Needle U.S. Size Range	1 to 3	3 to 5	5 to 7	7 to 9	9 to 11	11 and larger

* GUIDELINES ONLY: The above reflect the most commonly used gauges and needle sizes for specific yarn categories.

ribs

k1, p1 rib

▲ (multiple of 2 sts plus 1)

Row 1 (RS) K1, *pl, k1; rep from * to end.

Row 2 P1, *k1, pl; rep from * to end.

Rep rows 1 and 2 until desired length.

Cont as desired.

k1, p1 horizontal rib

▶ (multiple of 2 sts plus 1)

Cast on sts needed for desired width of rib.

Rep rows 1 and 2 of k1, p1 rib until piece measures width of piece, bind off.

Pick up and k along one side edge and cont as desired.

striped rib

▲ (multiple of 2 sts)

Row 1-6 With A *k1, p1; rep from * to end.

Row 7-10 With B *k1, p1; rep from * to end.

Row 11-18 With C *k1, p1; rep from * to end.

Row 19-22 With B *k1, p1; rep from * to end.

Cont as desired.

k1, p1 layered rib

▲ (multiple of 2 sts plus 1)

With A, cast on and work 2 rows in k1, p1 rib.

Change to B and work in rib until piece measures 2"/5cm. Place sts on spare needle.

With A, cast on and work 2 rows in k1, p1 rib.

Change to B and work in rib until piece measures 3"/7.5cm. Place sts on spare needle.

With shorter rib in front of longer rib, join using 3-needle joining technique.

Cont as desired.

k1, p1 rib with rolled edging (bound off)

▼ (multiple of 2 sts plus 1)

Work in k1, p1 rib until desired length.

Work in St st for 1"/2.5cm, or desired length of roll.

Bind off.

k1, p1 rib with rolled edging (cast on)

▲ (multiple of 2 sts plus 1)

Cast on desired number of stitches.

Work in St st for 1"/2.5cm, or desired length of roll.

Work in K1, P1 rib until desired length.

Cont as desired.

k1, p1 twisted rib

▲ (multiple of 2 sts plus 1)

Row 1 (RS) K1 tbl, *pl, k1 tbl; rep from * to end.

Row 2 P1, *k1, p1; rep from * to end.

Rep rows 1 and 2 until desired length.

Cont as desired.

two-color rib

▲ (over an odd number of sts)

Cast on with B.

Row 1 (RS) *K1 A, k1 B; rep from *, end k1 A.

Row 2 P1 A, *k1 B, p1 A; rep from * to end.

Row 3 *K1 A, p1 B; rep from *, end k1 A.

Rep rows 2 and 3 until desired length.

Cont as desired.

k1, p1 double broken rib

▲ (over an even number of sts)

Row 1 (RS) *K1, p1; rep from * to end.

Rep row 1 for 1"/2.5cm, end with a WS row.

Next row (RS) *P1, k1; rep from * to end.

Rep this row for 1"/2.5cm, end with a WS row.

Cont as desired.

slip stitch scallop

▲ (multiple of 6 sts plus 5)

Row 1 (RS) *[K1, p1] twice, k1, sl 1; rep from *, end [k1, p1] twice, k1.

Row 2 *[P1, k1] twice, p1, sl 1; rep from *, end [p1, k1] twice, p1.

Rep rows 1 and 2 twice more—6 rows.

Work in k1, p1 rib until desired length.

Cont as desired.

scallop edging with rib

▲ (beg as a multiple of 11 sts plus 2 and end as a multiple of 6 sts plus 2)

Row 1 (WS) Purl.

Row 2 K2, *k1 and sl back to LH needle, lift the next 8 sts on LH needle over this st and off needle, yo twice, k first st again, k2; rep from * to end.

Row 3 K1 *p2tog, drop extra loop, [k1, k1 tbl] twice in yo, p1; rep from *, end k1.

Work in k1, p1 rib until desired length or cont as desired.

k2, p2 basic rib

▲ (multiple of 4 sts plus 2)

Row 1 (RS) K2, *p2, k2; rep from * to end.

Row 2 P2, *k2, p2; rep from * to end.

Rep rows 1 and 2 until desired length.

Cont as desired.

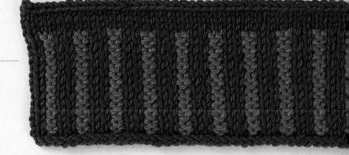

2 x 2 two color rib

▲ (multiple of 4 sts plus 2)

Cast on with A.

Row 1 (RS) *K2 A, k2 B; rep from *, end k2 A.

Row 2 P2 A, *k2 B, p2 A; rep from * to end.

Row 3 *K2 A, p2 B; rep from *, end k2 A.

Rep rows 2 and 3 until desired length.

Cont as desired.

corrugated rib

▲ (multiple of 6 sts plus 4)

Cast on with A.

Row 1 (RS) K1 A, *k2 B, k1 A, p2 B, k1 A; rep from * to end.

Row 2 P1 A, *p2 B, p1 A, k2 B, p1 A; rep from * to end.

Rep rows 1 and 2 until desired length.

Cont as desired.

basket rib I

▲ (multiple of 2 sts plus 1)

• Sl all sts purlwise.

Row 1 (RS) Knit.

Row 2 Purl.

Row 3 K1, *sl 1, k1; rep from * to end.

Row 4 K1, *sl 1 wyif, k1; rep from * to end.

Rep rows 1 to 4 until desired length.

Cont as desired.

basket rib II (2 color)

▲ Work as for **Basket Rib I**, working rows 1 and 2 with A and rows 2 and 3 with B until desired length.

Cont as desired.

basket rib III (3 color)

▲ Work as for **Basket Rib I**, working 2 rows each with A, B and C throughout until desired length.

Cont as desired.

supple rib

▲ (multiple of 3 sts)

Row 1 (RS) *K1, k the next st but keep on LH needle, p the same st tog with the next st; rep from * to end.

Row 2 Purl.

Rep rows 1 and 2 until desired length.

Cont as desired.

3 x 1 slip stitch rib

▲ (multiple of 4 sts)

Row 1 (RS) *K3, sl 1 purlwise; rep from * to end.

Row 2 Purl.

Rep rows 1 and 2 until desired length.

Cont as desired.

slipped rib I

▲ (multiple of 4 sts plus 3)

• Sl all sts purlwise.

Row 1 (RS) K1, sl 1, *k3, sl 1; rep from *, end k1.

Row 2 P1, sl 1, *p3, sl 1; rep from *, end p1.

Row 3 *K3, sl 1; rep from *, end k3.

Row 4 *P3, sl 1; rep from *, end p3.

Rep rows 1 to 4 until desired length.

Cont as desired.

slipped rib II

▲ Work as for **Slipped Rib I**, working 2 rows each in A, B and C throughout until desired length.

Cont as desired.

fancy slip stitch rib

▲ (multiple of 5 sts)

Row 1 (RS) *P2, k1, sl 1 purlwise, k1; rep from * to end.

Row 2 *P3, k2; rep from * to end.

Rep rows 1 and 2 until desired length.

Cont as desired.

double twisted rib

▲ (multiple of 6 sts)

Row 1 (RS) *P2, sl l, k1 keeping st on LH needle, pass sl st over, then k st again tbl, k tbl 2nd st on LH needle, pass it over the first st then k first st; rep from * to end.

Row 2 *P4, k2; rep from * to end.

Rep rows 1 and 2 until desired length.

Cont as desired.

hindu pillar stitch

▲ (multiple of 4 sts plus 1)

K 1 row.

Row 1 (RS) K1, *p3tog but do not drop sts, then k3tog and p3tog the same sts again, k1; rep from * to end.

Row 2 Purl.

Rep rows 1 and 2 until desired length.

Cont as desired.

maypole rib

▲ (multiple of 7 sts)

Row 1 (RS) *2-st LC, k3, p2; rep from * to end.

Row 2 and all WS rows *K2, p5; rep from * to end.

Row 3 *K1, 2-st LC, k2, p2; rep from * to end.

Row 5 *K2, 2-st LC, k1, p2; rep from * to end.

Row 7 *K3, 2-st LC, p2; rep from * to end.

Row 8 Rep row 2.

Rep rows 1 to 8 until desired length.

Cont as desired.

hunters rib

▲ (multiple of 11 sts plus 4)

Row 1 (RS) *P4, [k1 tbl, p1] 3 times, k1 tbl; rep from *, end p4.

Row 2 K4, *p1, [k1tbl, p1] 3 times, k4; rep from * to end.

Rep rows 1 and 2 until desired length.

Cont as desired.

basketweave rib

▲ (multiple of 19 sts)

Row 1 (RS) *P5, k2, p5, k1, 2-st RC 3 times; rep from * to end.

Row 2 *P1, 2-st RPC 3 times, k5, 2-st RPC, k5; rep from * to end.

Rep rows 1 and 2 until desired length.

Cont as desired.

7 x 3 flat rib

▲ (multiple of 10 sts plus 7)

Row 1 (RS) K7, *p3, k7; rep from * to end.

Row 2 P7, *k3, p7; rep from * to end.

Rep rows 1 and 2 until desired length.

Cont as desired.

stripe seed stitch

▲ (multiple of 11 sts plus 5)

Row 1 (RS) K5, *[k1, p1] 3 times, k5; rep from * to end.

Row 2 *P5, [p1, k1] 3 times; rep from *, end p5.

Rep rows 1 and 2 until desired length.

Cont as desired.

fence rib

▲ (multiple of 12 sts plus 5)

Work in k1, p1 rib for 1"/2.5cm or desired length, end with a WS row.

Row 1 (RS) *[K1, p1] twice, k1, p7; rep from *, end [k1, p1] twice, k1.

Row 2 K the knit sts and p the purl sts.

Rep rows 1 and 2 until desired length.

Cont as desired.

2-st fence

▲ (multiple of 8 sts plus 3)

Work in k1, p1 rib for 1"/2.5cm.

Row 1 (RS) *K1, p1, k1, p5; rep from *, end k1, p1, k1.

Row 2 *P1, k1, p1, k5; rep from *, end p1, k1, p1.

Rep rows 1 and 2 until desired length.

Cont as desired.

mock tassel rib

▲ (multiple of 7 sts plus 2)

Row 1 (RS) P2, *k1 tbl, [p1, k1 tbl] twice, p2; rep from * to end.

Row 2 K2, *p1 tbl, [k1, p1 tbl] twice, k2; rep from * to end.

Rep rows 1 and 2 for 2"/5cm, end with a WS row.

Row 3 P2, *sl next 5 sts to cn and wrap yarn counterclockwise around cn (snugly) 4 times, sl these 5 sts onto RH needle, p2; rep from * to end.

Row 4 K2, *p5, k2; rep from * to end.

Row 5 P2, *k5, p2; rep from * to end.

Row 6 K2, *1/1 RPC, p1, 1/1 LPC, k2; rep from * to end.

Row 7 P3, *M1, s2kp, M1, p4; rep from *, end last rep p3.

Row 8 K4, *p1, k6; rep from *, end last rep k4.

Row 9 P4, *k1, p6; rep from *, end last rep p4.

Row 10 Rep row 8.

Cont as desired.

bell tassel rib

▲ (multiple of 6 sts plus 1)

Rows 1, 3, 5, 7 and 9 (RS) *K4, p2; rep from *, end k1.

Rows 2, 4, 6, 8 and 10 P1,*k2, p4; rep from * to end.

Row 11 *Place RH needle between the 4th and 5th st and draw through a loop, k1, p2, k3; rep from *, end k1.

Row 12 P1 *p3, k2, p2tog; rep from * to end.

Cont as desired.

alternated ribs

▲ (multiple of 6 sts)

Row 1 (RS) *SK2P, p3; rep from * to end.

Row 2 *SK2P, [k1, k1 tbl, k1] in next st; rep from * to end.

Row 3 *P3, [k1, k1 tbl, k1] in next st; rep from * to end.

Rows 4, 5, 6, 7, 8, 9, 10, 11 and 12 *P3, k3; rep from * to end.

Row 13 *P3, SK2P; rep from * to end.

Row 14 *[K1, k1 tbl, k1] in next st, SP2P; rep from * to end.

Row 15 *[K1, k1 tbl, k1] in next st, p3; rep from * to end.

Rows 16 to 24 *K3, p3; rep from * to end.

Cont as desired.

broken basketweave rib

▲ (multiple of 4 sts plus 2)

Rows 1 and 3 (RS) *K2, p2; rep from *, end k2.

Row 2 and all WS rows K the knit sts and p the purl sts.

Rows 5 and 7 *P2, k2; rep from *, end p2.

Row 8 Rep row 2.

Rep rows 1 to 8 until desired length.

Cont as desired.

waffle st

▲ (multiple of 3 sts)

Rows 1 and 3 (RS) *K2, p1; rep from * to end.

Row 2 *K1, p2; rep from * to end.

Row 4 Knit.

Rep rows 1 to 4 until desired length.

Cont as desired.

pique rib

▲ (multiple of 10 sts)

Rows 1 and 3 (RS) *P3, k1, p3, k3; rep from * to end.

Row 2 *P3, k3, p1, k3; rep from * to end.

Row 4 Knit.

Rep rows 1 to 4 until desired length.

Cont as desired.

pillar rib

▲ (multiple of 3 sts)

Rows 1 and 3 (RS) *K1 tb1, k2; rep from * to end.

Rows 2 and 4 *P2, p1 tbl; rep from * to end.

Rows 5 and 7 *K1 tb1, p1, k1 tbl; rep from * to end.

Rows 6 and 8 *P1 tbl, k1, p1 tbl; rep from * to end.

Rows 9 and 11 *P2, k1 tb1; rep from * to end.

Rows 10 and 12 *P1 tbl, k2; rep from * to end.

Rep rows 1 to 12 once more.

Cont as desired.

zig-zag rib

▲ (multiple of 5 sts plus 2)

Rows 1, 3, 5, 7 and 9 (RS) K1 *p2tog, p1, M1, k2;
rep from *, end k1.

Row 2 and all WS rows Purl.

Rows 11, 13, 15, 17 and 19 K1, *M1, p2tog, p1, k2;
rep from *, end k1.

Row 20 Purl.

Rep rows 1 to 10 once more.

Cont as desired.

wavy rib

▲ (multiple of 6 sts)

Rows 1, 3 and 5 (RS) *P4, k2; rep from * to end.

Rows 2, 4 and 6 *P2, k4; rep from * to end.

Row 7 *P2, 2/2 RPC; rep from * to end.

Row 8, 10 and 12 K2,*p2, k4; rep from *, end last rep k2.

Rows 9 and 11 P2,*k2, p4; rep from *, end last rep p2.

Row 13 *2/2 RPC, p2; rep from * to end.

Rows 14 and 16 *K4, p2; rep from * to end.

Rows 15 and 17 *K2, p4; rep from * to end.

Row 18 Rep row 14.

Rep rows 1 to 18 until desired length.

Cont as desired.

diagonal wave rib

▲ (multiple of 6 sts plus 3)

Rows 1, 3 and 5 (RS) K3 *p3, k3; rep from * to end.

Rows 2 and 4 P3 *k3, p3; rep from * to end.

Row 6 *3/3 RPC; rep from *, end k3.

Rows 7, 9 and 11 P3, *k3, p3; rep from * to end.

Rows 8 and 10 K3, *p3, k3; rep from * to end.

Row 12 P3, *3/3 RPC; rep from * to end.

Cont as desired.

hanging rib

▲ (multiple of 8 sts)

Rows 1 and 3 (WS) *K3, sl 1 purlwise wyif, k3, p1; rep from * to end.

Row 2 *K1, p3, sl 1 purlwise wyib, p3; rep from * to end.

Row 4 *K1, p3; rep from * to end.

Rep rows 1 to 4 until desired length.

Cont as desired.

farrow rib

▲ (multiple of 3 sts)

Row 1 *K2, p1; rep from * to end.

Rep row 1 until desired length.

Cont as desired.

seed knit rib

▲ (multiple of 4 sts)

Row 1 (RS) *K3, p1; rep from * to end.

Row 2 *K2, p1, k1; rep from * to end.

Rep rows 1 and 2 until desired length.

Cont as desired.

double ricrac

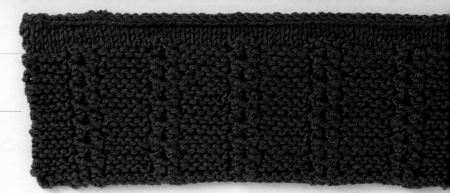

▲ (multiple of 9 sts plus 5)

Row 1 (RS) *P5, 2-st RC, 2-st LC; rep from *, end p5.

Row 2 *P5, k4; rep from *, end p5.

Row 3 *P5, 2-st LC, 2-st RC; rep from *, end p5.

Row 4 Rep row 2.

Rep rows 1 to 4 until desired length.

Cont as desired.

garter stitch rib

▲ (multiple of 6 sts)

Row 1 (WS) *K3, p3; rep from * to end.

Row 2 Knit.

Rep rows 1 and 2 until desired length.

Cont as desired.

mock rib

▲ (multiple of 2 sts)

Row 1 *P1, sl 1 purlwise wyib; rep from * to end.

Row 2 Purl.

Rep rows 1 and 2 until desired length.

Cont as desired.

embossed pyramid pattern

▲ (multiple of 8 sts plus 1)

Rows 1 and 3 (RS) *P1, k1 tbl; rep from *, end p1.

Rows 2 and 4 *K1, p1 tbl; rep from *, end k1.

Rows 5 and 7 *P2, [k1 tbl, p1] 3 times; rep from *, end p1.

Rows 6 and 8 *K2, [p1 tbl, k1] 3 times; rep from *, end k1.

Rows 9 and 11 *P3, k1 tbl, p1, k1 tbl, p2; rep from *, end p1.

Rows 10 and 12 *K3, p1 tbl, k1, p1 tbl, k2; rep from *, end k1.

Rows 13 and 15 *P4, k1 tbl, p3; rep from *, end p1.

Rows 14 and 16 *K4, p1 tbl, k3; rep from *, end k1.

Cont as desired.

chevron rib

▲ (multiple of 14 sts)

Row 1 (RS) *K1, p4, k4, p4, k1; rep from * to end.

Row 2 and all WS rows K the knit sts and p the purl sts.

Row 3 *K1, p3, k6, p3, k1; rep from * to end.

Row 5 *K1, p2, [k2, p1] twice, k2, p2, k1; rep from * to end.

Row 7 *K1, p1, [k2, p2] twice, k2, p1, k1; rep from * to end.

Row 9 *K3, p3, k2, p3, k3; rep from * to end.

Row 11 *K2, [p4, k2] twice; rep from * to end.

Row 13 K1, *p5, k2; rep from *, end last rep k1.

Row 14 Rep row 2.

Cont as desired.

triangular rib

▲ (multiple of 16 sts)

Rows 1 and 9 (RS) *K3, p1, k4, p3, k4, p1; rep from * to end.

Rows 2 and 8 *K2, p3, k3, p3, k2, p3; rep from * to end.

Rows 3 and 7 *K3, [p3, k2] twice, p3; rep from * to end.

Rows 4 and 6 *K4, p1, k3, p1, k4, p3; rep from * to end.

Row 5 *K3, p13; rep from * to end.

Row 10 *P5, k3, p8; rep from * to end.

Rep rows 1 to 10 once more.

Cont as desired.

loop st rib

▲ (multiple of 8 sts plus 4)

Row 1 (RS) *P4, [k1 wrapping yarn 3 times] 4 times; rep from *, end p4.

Row 2 K4, *sl 4 purlwise, letting the extra loops drop, k4; rep from * to end.

Row 3 *P4, sl 4 wyib; rep from *, end p4.

Row 4 K4, *sl 4 purlwise, k4; rep from * to end.

Rep rows 1 to 4 until desired length.

Cont as desired.

twin cable rib

▲ (multiple of 10 sts plus 3)

Row 1 (RS) *P3, k3, p1, k3; rep from *, end p3.

Row 2 K3, *p3, k1, p3, k3; rep from * to end.

Row 3 *P3, sl 1 purlwise, k2, p1, k2, sl 1 purlwise; rep from *, end p3.

Row 4 K3, *sl 1 purlwise, p2, k1, p2, sl 1 purlwise, k3; rep from * to end.

Row 5 *P3, 1/2 LC, p1, 2/1 RC; rep from * to end.

Row 6 Rep row 2.

Rep rows 1 to 6 until desired length.

Cont as desired.

corded rib

▲ (multiple of 5 sts plus 2)

Row 1 (RS) *P2, 2-st RC, k1; rep from *, end p2.

Row 2 K2, *p2, sl 1 purlwise, k2; rep from * to end.

Row 3 *P2, 2-st LC, k1; rep from *, end p2.

Row 4 K2, *p3, k2; rep from * to end.

Rep rows 1 to 4 until desired length.

Cont as desired.

baby cable rib

▲ (multiple of 4 sts plus 2)

Row 1 (RS) *P2, k2; rep from *, end p2.

Row 2 K2, *p2, k2; rep from * to end.

Row 3 *P2, RT; rep from *, end p2.

Row 4 Rep row 2.

Rep rows 1 to 4 until desired length.

Cont as desired.

pyramid baby cable rib

▲ (multiple of 4 sts plus 2)

Rep rows 1 to 4 of **Baby Cable Rib**, working
1 less cable each side every 4th row, working
these sts in St st.

Cont as desired.

single cable rib

▲ (multiple of 5 sts plus 3)

Rows 1 and 3 (RS) *P3, k2; rep from *, end p3.

Rows 2 and 4 K3, *p2, k3; rep from * to end.

Row 5 *P3, 2-st RC; rep from *, end p3.

Row 6 Rep row 2.

Rep rows 1 to 6 until desired length.

Cont as desired.

four stitch cable rib

▲ (multiple of 8 sts)

Row 1 (RS) *P2, k4, p2; rep from * to end.

Row 2 *K2, p4, k2; rep from * to end.

Row 3 *P2, 4-st LC, p2; rep from * to end.

Row 4 Rep row 2.

Rep rows 1 to 4 until desired length.

Cont as desired.

two color mock cable rib

▲ (multiple of 5 sts plus 2)

Cast on with A.

K 1 row.

Row 1 (RS) *P2 A, 2/1 RC B; rep from *, end p2 A.

Row 2 *K2 A, p3 B; rep from *, end k2 A.

Row 3 *P2 A, k3 B; rep from *, end p2 A.

Row 4 Rep row 2.

Rep rows 1 to 4 until desired length.

Cont as desired.

crossed rib

▲ (multiple of 5 sts)

Rows 1 and 3 (RS) *P1, [k1, p1] twice; rep from * to end.

Rows 2 and 4 *K1, [p1, k1] twice; rep from * to end.

Row 5 *P1, k the 3rd st, p the 2nd st, then k the first st, drop all 3 sts from LH needle, p1; rep from *, to end.

Row 6 Rep row 2.

Rep rows 1 to 6 until desired length.

Cont as desired.

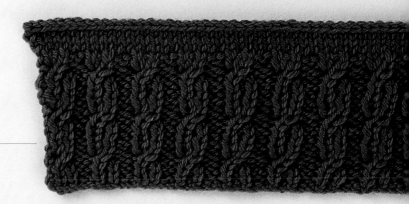

simple cable rib

▲ (multiple of 7 sts plus 3)

Rows 1 and 3 (RS) *P3, k4; rep from *, end p3.

Rows 2 and 4 *K3, p4; rep from *, end k3.

Row 5 *P3, 4-st LC; rep from *, end p3.

Row 6 Rep row 2.

Rep rows 1 to 6 until desired length.

Cont as desired.

twisted cable rib

▲ (multiple of 8 sts plus 3)

Row 1 (RS) *P3, k5; rep from *, end p3.

Rows 2 and 4 *K3, p5; rep from *, end k3.

Row 3 *P3, k1, 2-st RC twice; rep from *, end p3.

Row 5 *P3, 2-st RC twice, k1; rep from *, end p3.

Row 6 Rep row 2.

Rep rows 1 to 6 until desired length.

Cont as desired.

granite rib

▲ (multiple of 8 sts plus 2)

Row 1 (RS) *K2, 2-st RC 3 times; rep from *, end k2.

Row 2 Purl.

Row 3 *K2, 2/1 RC twice; rep from *, end k2.

Row 4 Rep row 2.

Rep rows 1 to 4 until desired length.

Cont as desired.

bell cable rib

▲ (multiple of 14 sts plus 2)

• On row 19 alternate 6-st RC and 6-st LC across row.

Rows 1, 3, 5, 7 and 9 (RS) *P2, k2, [p3, k2] twice; rep from *, end p2.

Row 2 and all WS rows K the knit sts and p the purl sts.

Row 11 *P2, 2/3 LPC, k2, 2/3 RPC; rep from *, end p2.

Rows 13, 15, and 17 P5, *k6, p8; rep from *, end last rep p5.

Row 19 P5, *6-st LC (see note), p8; rep from *, end last rep p5.

Rows 21 and 23 Rep row 13.

Row 24 Rep row 2.

Cont as desired.

embossed drop stitch

▲ (multiple of 9 sts)

Row 1 (RS) *P4, 2-st RC, p3; rep from * to end.

Row 2 *K3, p1, M1 p-st, p1, k4; rep from * to end.

Rows 3, 5, 7 and 9 *P4, k3, p3; rep from * to end.

Rows 4, 6 and 8 *K3, p3, k4; rep from * to end.

Row 10 *K3, p1, drop next st, p1, k4; rep from * to end.

Rep rows 1 to 10 until desired length.

Cont as desired.

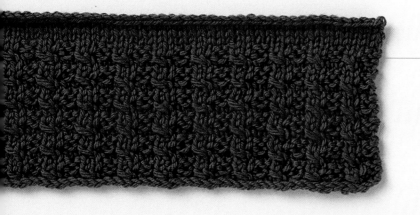

horizontal twist rib

▲ (multiple of 4 sts plus 2)

Row 1 Knit.

Row 2 Purl.

Row 3 *P2, LT; rep from *, end p2.

Row 4 K2, *p2, k2; rep from * to end.

Rep rows 1 to 4 until desired length.

Cont as desired.

flagon stitch

▲ (multiple of 6 sts)

Row 1 and all WS rows *P2, k1; rep from * to end.

Rows 2, 4, 6 and 8 *P1, k2, p1, sl 1 purlwise wyib, p1, yo, pass the sl st over the p1 and yo.

Rows 10, 12, 14 and 16 *P1, sl 1 purlwise wyib, p1, yo, pass the sl st over the p1 and yo, p1, k2; rep from * to end.

Rep rows 1 to 16 until desired length.

Cont as desired.

ribbed cables

▲ (multiple of 5 sts)

Row 1 (RS) *P4, [k1, k1 tbl, k1] in next st; rep from * to end.

Row 2 *P3, k4; rep from * to end.

Row 3 *P4, k3tog; rep from * to end.

Row 4 *P1, k4; rep from * to end.

Rep rows 1 to 4 until desired length.

Cont as desired.

seed stitch cable

▲ (multiple of 9 st plus 5)

Rows 1 and 3 (WS) [K1, p1] twice, k1, *k1 tbl, p2, k1 tbl, [k1, p1] twice, k1; rep from * to end.

Rows 2 and 4 *[K1, p1] 3 times, k2, p1; rep from *, end [k1, p1] twice, k1.

Row 5 [K1, p1] twice, k1, *yo, k1, p2, k1, sl yo over 4 sts, [k1, p1] twice, k1; rep from * to end.

Row 6 Rep row 2.

Rep rows 1 to 6 until desired length.

Cont as desired.

candy twist cable

▲ (multiple of 15 sts plus 5)

Rows 1, 3 and 7 (RS) Knit.

Row 2 and all WS rows K2, p1, *k4, p6, k4, p1; rep from *, end k2.

Rows 5, 9 and 13 K7, 6-st RC, *k9, 6-st RC; rep from *, end k7.

Rows 11, 15, 17, 19, 21 and 23 Knit.

Row 24 Rep row 2.

Rep rows 1 to 14 once more.

Cont as desired.

alternating cable rib

▲ (multiple of 9 sts plus 3)

Row 1 (RS) *P3, k6; rep from *, end p3.

Row 2 and all WS rows *K3, p6; rep from *, end k3.

Row 3 *P3, 4-st RC, k2; rep from *, end p3.

Row 5 *P3, k2, 4-st LC; rep from *, end p3.

Row 6 Rep row 2.

Rep rows 1 to 6 until desired length.

Cont as desired.

twin cable rib

▲ (multiple of 11 sts plus 2)

Rows 1 and 3 (RS) *P2, k9; rep from *, end p2.

Rows 2 and 4 *K2, p4, k1, p4; rep from *, end k2.

Row 5 *P2, 4-st RC, k1, 4-st LC; rep from *, end p2.

Row 6 Rep row 2.

Rep rows 1 to 6 until desired length.

Cont as desired.

reverse cable rib

▲ (multiple of 11 sts plus 3)

Rows 1 and 3 (RS) *P3, k8; rep from *, end p3.

Rows 2 and 4 *K3, p8; rep from *, end k3.

Row 5 *P3, 4-st RC, 4-st LC; rep from *, end p3.

Row 6 Rep row 2.

Rep rows 1 to 6 until desired length.

Cont as desired.

sycamore stitch

▲ (multiple of 12 sts plus 4)

Rows 1, 3 and 5 (RS) P4, *k2, p4; rep from * to end.

Rows 2 and 4 K4, *p2, k4; rep from * to end.

Row 6 K4, *sl 2 purlwise wyif, k4; rep from * to end.

Row 7 P4, *sl 2 to cn and hold to front, p2, yo, k2tog tbl from cn, sl 2 to cn and hold to back, k2tog, yo, p2 from cn, p4; rep from * to end.

Row 8 K4, *p2, k1 tbl, k2, k1 tbl, p2, k4; rep from * to end.

Rep rows 1 to 8 until desired length.

Cont as desired.

six stitch plait rib

▲ (multiple of 9 sts plus 3)

Row 1 (RS) P3, *4-st LC, k2, p3; rep from * to end.

Row 2 *K3, p6; rep from *, end k3.

Row 3 P3, *k2, 4-st RC, p3; rep from * to end.

Row 4 Rep row 2.

Rep rows 1 to 4 until desired length.

Cont as desired.

snakey cable

▲ (multiple of 7 sts plus 3)

Rows 1 and 3 (RS) *P3, k4; rep from *, end p3.

Rows 2 all WS rows *K3, p4; rep from *, end k3.

Row 5 *P3, 4-st RC; rep from *, end p3.

Rows 7 and 9 Rep row 1.

Row 11 *P3, 4-st LC; rep from *, end p3.

Row 12 Rep row 2.

Rep rows 1 to 12 until desired length.

Cont as desired.

open twisted rib

▲ (multiple of 5 sts plus 3)

Row 1 (RS) *P1, k1 tbl, p1, k2; rep from *, end p1, k1 tbl, p1.

Row 2 K1, p1 tbl, k1, *p2, k1, p1 tbl, k1; rep from * to end.

Row 3 *P1, k1 tbl, p1, k1, yo, k1; rep from *, end p1, k1 tbl, p1.

Row 4 K1, p1 tbl, k1, *p3, k1, p1 tbl, k1; rep from * to end.

Row 5 *P1, k1 tbl, p1, k3, pass 3rd st on RH needle over first 2 sts; rep from *, end p1, k1 tbl, p1.

Rep rows 2 to 5 until desired length.

Cont as desired.

2 x 2 and two stitch cable rib

▲ (multiple of 8 sts plus 6)

Row 1 (RS) *P2, k2; rep from *, end p2.

Row 2 *K2, p2; rep from *, end k2.

Row 3 *P2, k2, p2, RT; rep from *, end p2, k2, p2.

Row 4 Rep row 2.

Rep rows 1 to 4 until desired length.

Cont as desired.

circle rib

▲ (multiple of 10 sts plus 2)

Row 1 (RS) K2 *p2, RT, LT, p2, k2; rep from * to end.

Row 2 *P2, k2, p4, k2; rep from *, end p2.

Row 3 K2, *p2, LT, RT, p2, k2; rep from * to end.

Row 4 Rep row 2.

Rep rows 1 to 4 until desired length.

Cont as desired.

cable and bar rib

▲ (multiple of 10 sts plus 8)

Rows 1 and 5 (RS) *P2, k4, p2, 2-st LC; rep from *, end p2, k4, p2.

Rows 2 and 4 *K2, p4, k2, p2; rep from *, end k2, p4, k2.

Row 3 *P2, 4-st LC, p2, 2-st LC; rep from *, end p2, 4-st LC, p2.

Row 6 Rep row 2.

Rep rows 1 to 6 until desired length.

Cont as desired.

1 x 1 rib and cable combination

▲ (multile of 9 sts plus 5)

Row 1 (RS) *[P1, k1] twice, p1, k4; rep from *, end p1, [k1, p1] twice.

Row 2 *[K1, p1] twice, k1, p4; rep from *, end [k1, p1] twice, k1.

Row 3 *[P1, k1] twice, p1, 4-st RC; rep from *, end p1, [k1, p1] twice.

Row 4 Rep row 2.

Rep rows 1 to 4 until desired length.

Cont as desired.

2 x 2 rib with double four-stitch cables

▲ (multiple of 20 sts plus 6)

Row 1 (RS) *[K2, p2] twice, [k4, p2] twice; rep from *, end k2, p2, k2.

Row 2 *[P2, k2] twice, [p4, k2] twice, rep from *, end p2, k2, p2.

Row 3 *[K2, p2] twice, [4-st LC, p2] twice; rep from *, end k2, p2, k2.

Row 4 Rep row 2.

Rep rows 1 to 4 until desired length.

Cont as desired.

alternating link rib

▲ (multiple of 7 sts plus 4)

Rows 1 and 3 (RS) *P5, k1, p1; rep from *, end p4.

Row 2 and all WS rows K the knit sts and p the purl sts.

Rows 5 and 7 *P4, k1, p1, k1; rep from *, end p4.

Row 8 Rep row 2.

Rep rows 1 to 8 until desired length, end with row 4.

Cont as desired.

chain stitch

▲ (multiple of 8 sts plus 4)

K 1 row, p 1 row.

Row 1 (RS) *P4, 2-st LC, 2-st RC; rep from *, end p4.

Row 2 *K4, p4; rep from *, end k4.

Rows 3 and 5 *P4, k1, p2, k1; rep from *, end p4.

Rows 4 and 6 *K4, p1, k2, p1; rep from *, end k4.

Rep rows 1 to 6 until desired length.

Cont as desired.

braid stitch

▲ (multiple of 10 sts)

Row 1 (RS) *P3, k5, p2; rep from * to end.

Rows 2 and 4 *K2, p5, k3; rep from * to end.

Row 3 *P3, M1, k1, p3tog, k1, M1, p2; rep from * to end.

Rep rows 1 to 4 until desired length.

Cont as desired.

hurdle rib

▲ (multiple of 2 sts)

Rows 1 and 2 Knit.

Rows 3 and 4 *K1, p1: rep from * to end.

Rep rows 1 to 4 until desired length.

Cont as desired.

esparto stitch

▲ (multiple of 2 sts)

Row 1 (RS) *K 2nd st wrapping yarn twice round needle, k first st letting both sts drop from LH needle; rep from * to end.

Row 2 *P 2nd st wrapping yarn twice, p first letting both sts drop from LH needle; rep from * to end.

Rep rows 1 and 2 until desired length.

Cont as desired.

broken rib diagonal

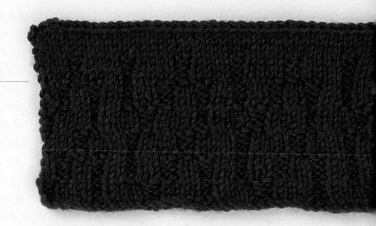

▲ (multiple of 12 sts)

Rows 1 and 3 (RS) *K4, p2; rep from * to end.

Row 2 and all WS rows K the purl sts and p the knit sts.

Rows 5 and 7 *K2, p2; rep from * to end.

Rows 9 and 11 *P2, k4; rep from * to end.

Row 12 Rep row 2.

Rep rows 1 to 12 until desired length.

Cont as desired.

oblique rib

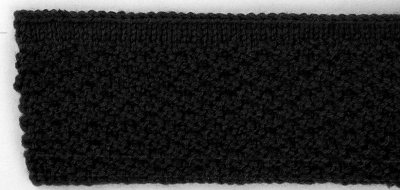

▲ (multiple of 4 sts)

Row 1 (RS) *K2, p2; rep from * to end.

Row 2 *K1, p2, k1; rep from * to end.

Row 3 *P2, k2; rep from * to end.

Row 4 *P1, k2, p1; rep from * to end.

Rep rows 1 to 4 until desired length.

Cont as desired.

caliper cables

▲ (multiple of 13 sts plus 3)

Rows 1 and 3 (WS) K3 *p1 wrapping yarn twice, p8, p1 wrapping yarn twice, k3; rep from * to end.

Rows 2 and 4 P3, *drop next st and extra wraps, k4, pick up and k dropped st, sl 4 wyib, drop next st and extra wraps, sl the 4 sts back to LH needle, pick up and k dropped st, k4, p3; rep from * to end.

Row 5 K3, *p10, k3; rep from * to end.

Row 6 P3, *k10, p3; rep from * to end.

Rep rows 1 to 6 until desired length, end with row 4.

Cont as desired.

elongated caliper cables

▲ (multiple of 13 sts plus 3)

Rep rows 1 and 2 only of **Caliper Cables** until desired length.

Cont as desired.

criss-cross

▲ (multiple of 6 sts plus 1)

Rows 1, 7 and 9 K1 tbl, *k1, p3, k1, k1 tbl; rep from * to end.

Rows 2, 6 and 8 P1 tbl, *p1, k3, p1, pl tbl; rep from * to end.

Row 3 K1 tbl, *sl 1, p3, sl 1, k1 tbl; rep from * to end.

Row 4 P1 tbl, *sl 1, k3, sl 1, p1 tbl; rep from * to end.

Row 5 K1 tbl, *5-st RLC, k1 tbl; rep from * to end.

Row 10 Rep row 2.

Rep rows 1 to 10 until desired length.

Cont as desired.

1 x 1 and spiral rib combo

▲ (multiple of 13 sts plus 7)

Row 1 (RS) P1, [k1, p1] 3 times, *RT 3 times, [p1, k1] 3 times, p1; rep from * to end.

Row 2 [K1, p1] 3 times, k1, *p6, [k1, p1] 3 times, k1; rep from * to end.

Row 3 P1, [k1, p1] 3 times, *k1, RT twice, [k1, p1] 4 times; rep from * to end.

Row 4 Rep row 2.

Rep rows 1 to 4 until desired length.

Cont as desired.

2 x 2 rib with traveling cables

▲ (multiple of 18 sts plus 6)

Row 1 (RS) *K2, p2, k2, p3, 2-st RC, p2, 2-st RC, p3; rep from *, end k2, p2, k2.

Row 2, 4 and 6 K the knit sts and p the purl sts.

Row 3 *[K2, p2] twice, [1/1 RPC, 1/1 LPC] twice, p2; rep from *, end k2, p2, k2.

Row 5 *[K2, p2] twice, k1, p2, 2-st LC, p2, k1,

p2; rep from *, end k2, p2, k2,

Row 7 *[K2, p2] twice, [1/1 LPC, 1/1 RPC] twice, p2; rep from *, end k2, p2, k2.

Row 8 Rep row 2.

Rep rows 1 to 8 until desired length.

Cont as desired.

1 x 1 woven diamond rib

▲ (multiple of 19 sts plus 3)

• K all k sts tbl on RS and p all p sts tbl on WS.

• Work all cables in reverse on WS rows as foll: 1/1 RC is worked as 2 k sts on the RS and as 2 p sts on the WS. The direction that the sts move rem the same.

Rows 1, 3, 5, 19, 21 and 23 (RS) P1, k3 tbl, *[p1, k1 tbl] twice, p2, RT, p2, [k1 tbl, p1] twice, k5 tbl; rep from *, end last rep k3 tbl, p1.

Rows 2, 4, 6, 18, 20 and 22 K1, p3 tbl, *[k1, p1 tbl] twice, k2, p2, k2, [p1 tbl, k1] twice, p5 tbl; rep from *, end last rep p3 tbl, k1.

Row 7 P1, k3 tbl, *p1, k1 tbl, p1, [1/1 LPC, 1/1 RPC] twice, p1, k1 tbl, p1, k5 tbl; rep from *, end last rep k3 tbl, p1.

Row 8 K1, p3 tbl, *k1, p1 tbl, k2, [2-st LC, k2] twice, p1 tbl, k1, p5 tbl; rep from *, end last rep p3 tbl, k1.

Rows 9 and 13 P1, k3 tbl, *p1, [1/1 LPC, 1/1 RPC]

3 times, p1, k5 tbl; rep from *, end last rep k3 tbl, p1.

Rows 10 and 14 K1, p3 tbl, *[k2, 2-st RC] 3 times, k2, p5 tbl; rep from *, end last rep p3 tbl, k1.

Rows 11 and 15 P1, k3 tbl, *p1, [1/1 RPC, 1/1 LPC] 3 times, p1, k5 tbl; rep from *, end last rep k3 tbl, p1.

Row 12 K1, p3 tbl, *k1, p1 tbl, [k2, 2-st LC] twice, k2, p1 tbl, k1, p5 tbl; rep from *, end last rep p3 tbl, k1.

Row 16 K1, p3 tbl, *k1, p1 tbl, [k2, 2-st LC] twice, k2, p1 tbl, k1, p5 tbl; rep from *, end last rep p3 tbl, k1.

Row 17 P1, k3 tbl, *p1, k1 tbl, p1, [1/1 RPC, 1/1 LPC] twice, p1, k1 tbl, p1, k5 tbl; rep from *, end last rep k3 tbl, p1.

Row 24 Rep row 2.

Rep rows 1 to 7 once more.

Cont as desired.

jump the broom

▲ (multiple of 14 sts plus 1)

Row 1 (WS) K1, *p2, [k1, p1 tbl] 4 times, k1, p2, k1; rep from * to end.

Row 2 *P1, 2/1 LC, [k1 tbl, p1] 3 times, k1 tbl, 1/2 RC; rep from *, end p1.

Row 3 K1, *p1 tbl, p2, [p1 tbl, k1] 3 times, p1 tbl, p2, p1 tbl, k1; rep from * to end.

Row 4 *P1, k1 tbl, 2/1 LPC, [p1, k1 tbl] twice, p1, 1/2 RPC, k1 tbl; rep from *, end p1.

Row 5 K1, *p1 tbl, k1, p2, [k1, p1 tbl] twice, k1, p2, k1, p1 tbl, k1; rep from * to end.

Row 6 *P1, k1 tbl, p1, 2/1 LC, k1 tbl, p1, k1 tbl, 1/2 RC, p1, k1 tbl; rep from *, end p1.

Row 7 K1, *[p1 tbl, k1, p1 tbl, p2] twice, [p1 tbl, k1] twice; rep from * to end.

Row 8 *[P1, k1 tbl] twice, 2/1 LPC, p1, 1/2 RPC, k1 tbl, p1, k1 tbl; rep from *, end p1.

Row 9 K1, *[p1 tbl, k1] twice, p2, k1, p2, [k1, p1 tbl] twice, k1; rep from * to end.

Row 10 *[P1, k1 tbl] twice, p1, 3/2 RTC, [p1, k1 tbl] twice; rep from *, end p1.

Row 11 K1, *[p1 tbl, k1] twice, p2, k1, p2, [k1, p1 tbl] twice, k1; rep from * to end.

Row 12 *[P1, k1 tbl] twice, p1, k2, p1, k2, [p1, k1 tbl] twice; rep from *, end p1.

Row 13 K1, *[p1 tbl, k1] twice, p2, k1, p2, [k1, p1 tbl] twice, k1; rep from * to end.

Row 14 *[P1, k1 tbl] twice, p1, 3/2 RTC, [p1, k1 tbl] twice; rep from *, end p1.

Row 15, 17, 19 and 21 K1, *[p1 tbl, k1] twice, p2, k1, p2, [k1, p1 tbl] twice, k1; rep from * to end.

Rows 16, 18 and 20 *[P1, k1 tbl] twice, p1, k2, p1, k2, [p1, k1 tbl] twice; rep from *, end p1.

Cont as desired.

k1, p1 rib and cable block

▲ (multiple of 24 sts plus 13)

Rows 1, 3, 5, 9 and 11 K1, *k13, [p2, k1] 3 times, p2; rep from *, end k14.

Row 2 and all WS rows K the knit sts and p the purl sts.

Row 7 K1, *3/3 RC, k1, 3/3 RC, [p2, k1] 3 times, p2; rep from *, end [3/3 RC, k1] twice.

Rows 13, 15, 17, 21 and 23 K2, *[p2, k1] 3 times, p2, k13; rep from *, end [p2, k1] 4 times, k1.

Row 19 K2, *[p2, k1] 3 times, p2, 3/3 RC, k1, 3/3 RC; rep from *, end [p2, k1] 4 times, k1.

Rep rows 1 to 24 until desired length.

Cont as desired.

cross box

▲ (multiple of 16 sts plus 8)

K 4 rows.

Rows 1, 3 and 5 (RS) P1, k6, *p4, k2, p4, k6; rep from *, end p1.

Rows 2 and 4 K11, p2, *k14, p2; rep from *, end k11.

Row 6 K1, p6, *k4, p2, k4, p6; rep from *, end k1.

Row 7 P3, k2, *2/2 LPC, p2, k2, p2, 2/2 RPC, k2; rep from *, end p3.

Row 8 K3, p2, *k2, p2; rep from *, end k3.

Row 9 P3, k2, *p2, 2/2 LPC, k2, 2/2 RPC, p2, k2; rep from *, end p3.

Row 10 K3, p2, *k4, p6, k4, p2; rep from *, end k3.

Rows 11, 13 and 15 P3, k2, *p4, k6, p4, k2; rep from *, end p3.

Rows 12 and 14 K3, p2, *k14, p2; rep from *, end k3.

Rows 16 and 18 Rep row 10.

Row 17 P3, k2, *p4, 6-st RC, p4, k2; rep from *, end p3.

Rows 19, 21 and 23 Rep row 11.

Rows 20 and 22 Rep row 12.

Row 24 Rep row 10.

Row 25 P3, k2, *p2, 2/2 RPC, k2, 2/2 LPC, p2, k2; rep from *, end p3.

Row 26 Rep row 8.

Row 27 P3, k2, *2/2 RPC, p2, k2, p2, 2/2 LPC, k2; rep from *, end p3.

Row 28 Rep row 6.

K 4 rows.

Cont as desired.

1 x 2 rib to v-point

▲ (multiple of 27 sts plus 2)

Work 2 rows in p2, k1 rib.

Row 1 (RS) P1, *k3, p1, [k1, p2] 6 times, k1, p1, k3; rep from *, end p1.

Row 2 and all WS rows K the knit sts and p the purl sts.

Row 3 P1, *3/1 LPC, [k1, p2] 6 times, k1, 3/1 RPC; rep from *, end p1.

Row 5 P1, *p1, 3/1 LPC, [p2, k1] 5 times, p2, 3/1 RPC, p1; rep from *, end p1.

Row 7 P1, *p2, 3/1 LPC, p1, [k1, p2] 4 times, k1, p1, 3/1 RPC, p2; rep from *, end p1.

Row 9 P1, *p3, 3/1 LPC, [k1, p2] 4 times, k1, 3/1 RPC, p3; rep from *, end p1.

Row 11 P1, *p4, 3/1 LPC, [p2, k1] 3 times, p2, 3/1 RPC, p4; rep from *, end p1.

Row 13 P1, *p5, 3/1 LPC, p1, [k1, p2] twice, k1, p1, 3/1 RPC, p5; rep from *, end p1.

Row 15 P1, *p6, 3/1 LPC, [k1, p2] twice, k1, 3/1 RPC, p6; rep from *, end p1.

Row 17 P1, *p7, 3/1 LPC, p2, k1, p2, 3/1 RPC, p7; rep from *, end p1.

Row 19 P1, *p8, 3/1 LPC, p1, k1, p1, 3/1 RPC, p8; rep from *, end p1.

Row 21 P1, *p9, 3/1 LPC, k1, 3/1 RPC, p9; rep from *, end p1.

Row 23 P1, *p10, M1 p-st, k2, s2kp, k2, M1 p-st, p10; rep from *, end p1.

Row 25 P1, *p11, M1 p-st, k1, s2kp, k1, M1 p-st, p11; rep from *, end p1.

Row 27 P1, *p12, M1 p-st, s2kp, M1 p-st, p12; rep from *, end p1.

Row 28 Knit.

Cont as desired.

k1, p1 graduated rib

▲ (beg as a multiple of 12 sts plus 3 and end as a multiple of 14 sts plus 3)

Row 1 (RS) K2, *p1, k1; rep from *, end k1.

Row 2 P2, *k1, p1; rep from *, end p1.

Rep rows 1 and 2 for 1"/2.5cm or desired length, end with row 1.

Inc row (WS) P2, *M1 p-st, rib 11 sts, M1 p-st, p1; rep from *, end p1.

Row 3 K2, *2-st LC, rib 9 sts, 2-st RC, k1; rep from *, end k1.

Rows 4, 6, 8 and 10 K the knit sts and p the purl sts.

Row 5 K3, *2-st LC, rib 7 sts, 2-st RC, k3; rep from * to end.

Row 7 K2, *2-st LC twice, rib 5 sts, 2-st RC twice, k1; rep from *, end k1.

Row 9 K3, *2-st LC twice, rib 3 sts, 2-st RC twice, k3; rep from * to end.

Row 11 K2, *2-st LC 3 times, k1, 2-st RC 3 times, k1; rep from *, end k1.

Cont as desired.

spirals

(Panel of 12 sts)

Row 1 K1, p2, RT 3 times, p2, k1.

Row 2 P1, k2, p6, k2, p1.

Row 3 K1, p2, k1, RT twice, k1, p2, k1.

Row 4 Rep row 2.

Rep rows 1 to 4 until desired length.

Cont as desired.

diamonds

▲ (Panel of 14 sts)

Row 1 (RS) P6, RT, p6.

Row 2 K6, p2, k6.

Row 3 P5, 1/1 RPC, 1/1 LPC, p5.

Row 4 K5, p1, k2, p1, k5.

Row 5 P4, 1/1 RPC, p2, 1/1 LPC, p4.

Row 6 K4, p1, k4, p1, k4.

Row 7 P3, 1/1 RPC, p1, RT, p1, 1/1 LPC, p3.

Row 8 K3, p1, k2, p2, k2, p1, k3.

Row 9 P2, 1/1 RPC, p1, 1/1 RPC, 1/1 LPC, p1, 1/1 LPC, p2.

Row 10 [K2, p1] 4 times, k2.

Row 11 P1, 1/1 RPC, p1, 1/1 RPC, p2, 1/1 LPC, p1, 1/1 LPC, p1.

Rows 12 and 14 K1, p1, k2, p1, k4, p1, k2, p1, k1.

Row 13 P1, k1, p2, k1, p4, k1, p2, k1, p1.

Row 15 P1, 1/1 LPC, p1, 1/1 LPC, p2, 1/1 RPC, p1, 1/1 RPC, p1.

Row 16 Rep row 10.

Row 17 P2, 1/1 LPC, p1, 1/1 LPC, 1/1 RPC, p1, 1/1 RPC, p2.

Row 18 Rep row 8.

Row 19 P3, 1/1 LPC, p1, 1/1 LPC, p1, 1/1 RPC, p3.

Row 20 Rep row 6.

Row 21 P4, 1/1 LPC, p2, 1/1 RPC, p4.

Row 22 Rep row 4.

Row 23 P5, 1/1 LPC, 1/1 RPC, p5.

Row 24 Rep row 2.

Rep rows 1 to 24 until desired length.

Cont as desired.

diamonds   spirals

tutti twists

▲ (multiple of 14 sts plus 10)

P 1 row.

Row 1 (WS) K1, p1, *k2, p2, k2, p1; rep from *, end k1.

Row 2 P3, 1/1 RPC, *[1/1 LPC, p1] twice, k2, [p1, 1/1 RPC] twice; rep from *, end 1/1 LPC, p3.

Rows 3 and 17 K2, *k1, p1, [k2, p1] twice, k1, p2, k1, p1, k1; rep from *, end k1, p1, k2, p1, k3.

Row 4 P2, 1/1 RPC, p2, 1/1 LPC, *p1, 1/1 LPC, k2, 1/1 RPC, p1, 1/1 RPC, p2, 1/1 LPC; rep from *, end p2.

Rows 5 and 15 K2, p1, k4, p1, k2, *p4, k2, p1, k4, p1, k2; rep from * to end.

Row 6 P1, 1/1 RPC, p4, 1/1 LPC, *p1, k4, p1, 1/1 RPC, p4, 1/1 LPC; rep from *, end p1.

Row 7 and 13 K1, p1, k6, p1, k1, *p4, k1, p1, k6, p1, k1; rep from * to end.

Row 8 P8, *1/1 LPC, k4, 1/1 RPC, p6; rep from *, end p2.

Rows 9 and 11 K9 *p6, k8; rep from *, end k1.

Row 10 P9, *6-st RC, p8; rep from *, end p1.

Row 12 P8, *1/1 RPC, k4, 1/1 LPC, p6; rep from *, end p2.

Row 14 P1, 1/1 LPC, p4, 1/1 RPC, *p1, k4, p1, 1/1 LPC, p4, 1/1 RPC; rep from *, end p1.

Row 16 P2, 1/1 LPC, p2, 1/1 RPC, *p1, 1/1 RPC, k2, 1/1 LPC, p1, 1/1 LPC, p2, 1/1 RPC; rep from *, end p2.

Row 18 P3, 1/1 LPC, *[1/1 RPC, p1] twice, k2, [p1, 1/1 LPC] twice; rep from *, end 1/1 RPC, p3.

Row 19 Rep row 1.

P 1 row.

Cont as desired.

diamond with chain

▲ (panel of 16 sts)

Row 1 (WS) K6, p4, k6.

Row 2 P5, 1/2 RPC, 2/1 LPC, p5.

Rows 3 and all WS rows K the knit sts and p the purl sts.

Row 4 P4, 1/2 RPC, k2, 2/1 LPC, p4.

Row 6 P3, 1/2 RPC, p1, 2-st RC, p1, 2/1 LPC, p3.

Row 8 P2, 1/2 RPC, p1, 1/1 RPC, 1/1 LPC, p1, 2/1 LPC, p2.

Row 10 P1, 1/2 RPC, p2, [k1, p2] twice, 2/1 LPC, p1.

Row 12 1/2 RPC, p3, 1/1 LPC, 1/1 RPC, p3, 2/1 LPC.

Row 14 K2, p5, 2-st RC, p5, k2.

Row 16 2/1 LPC, p3, 1/1 RPC, 1/1 LPC, p3, 1/2 RPC.

Row 18 P1, 2/1 LPC, p2, [k1, p2] twice, 1/2 RPC, p1.

Row 20 P2, 2/1 LPC, p1, 1/1 LPC, 1/1 RPC, p1, 1/2 RPC, p2.

Row 22 P3, 2/1 LPC, p1, 2-st RC, p1, 1/2 RPC, p3.

Row 24 P4, 2/1 LPC, p2, 1/2 RPC, p4.

Row 26 P5, 2/1 LPC, 1/2 RPC, p5.

Row 28 P6, 4-st RC, p6.

Cont as desired.

bobbled cable

▲ (panel of 11 sts)

Make Bobble (MB)

[k1, yo, k1, yo, k1] in next st—5 sts, turn, k5, turn, p5, turn, ssk, k1, k2tog, turn, p3tog.

Note: For a right-twist cable, work row 2 with a 7-st RC; for a left-twist cable work row 2 with a 7-st LC.

Rows 1 and all WS rows P1, k2, p7, k2, p1.

Row 2 K1, p2, work cable, p2, k1.

Rows 4, 6, 10 and 12 K1, p2, k7, p2, k1.

Row 8 Rep row 2.

Row 14 K1, p2, k3, MB, k3, p2, k1.

Row 16 Rep row 4.

Rep rows 1 to 16 until same length as Diamond with Chain.

Cont as desired.

bobbles   **diamonds**

ruffles

Varying Multiples

In this chapter, the number of stitches that you begin with to create the ruffle is different than the number that you will need at the end for desired measurement, or vice versa. Some are as simple as doubling or tripling the number of stitches that will be needed for the desired measurement. When working with small multiple repeats (or no repeats, as in garter stitch), you may need to eliminate or add a few stitches after the increasing or decreasing in order to get the final count.

basic knit 2 together gathered ruffle

▲ (Cast on double the amount of sts needed)

Work in St st (or desired pat) until desired length, end with a WS row.

For even number of sts:

Next (dec) row (RS) K2tog across.

For odd number of sts:

Next (dec) row (RS) K1, k2tog across.

Cont as desired.

basic knit 3 together gathered ruffle

▲ (Cast on 3 times the amount of sts needed)

Work in St st (or desired pat) until desired length, end with a WS row.

Next (dec) row (RS) K3tog across.

Cont as desired.

layered ruffle

▲ (Cast on double the amount of sts needed–beg with a multiple of 4 sts plus 1 and end with a multiple of 2 sts plus 1)

Bottom layer

Work in garter st for 2 rows.

Beg with WS row and work in St st until piece measures 2½"/6cm from beg, end with a WS row.

Next (dec) row (RS) K1, *k3tog, k1; rep from * to end. Place sts on a spare needle.

Top layer

Work as for bottom layer until piece measures 1"/2.5cm, end with a WS row.

Rep dec row.

Join layers

Purl, using the 3-needle joining technique.

Cont as desired.

When more intricate multiples are involved, it will be necessary to calculate the amount of stitches needed to increase or decrease using the given multiples to achieve the desired measurement. For example, using the Eyelet Point Ruffle on page 56, first determine the number of stitches needed after the ruffle is complete. Let's say you need 107 stitches. Multiply this number by 3 to get 321 stitches. Determine the closest multiple of 14 sts plus 1 by dividing 321 by 14 which equals 22.9. Therefore, if you work the 14-st rep 23 times you get 322 sts plus 1 equals 323 to cast on, which is just two stitches different from what you need. You can decrease these two on your first row above the ruffle.

simple stripe rib

▼ (multiple of 2 sts plus 1)

Stripe Pat

4 rows A, *2 rows B, 2 rows A; rep from * (4 rows) for stripe pat.

With A, work in k1, p1 rib until desired length.

Next (inc) row 1 (RS) *K1, inc 1; rep from *, end k1.

Row 2 Purl.

Cont in St st and stripe pat until desired length, end with a WS row.

K 3 rows A.

Bind off.

garter stitch ruffle

▼ (multiple of 2 sts plus 1)

• Use 2 different size needles. Begin with smaller needles.

Rows 1, 2 and 3 Knit.

Row 4 K1, *yo, k1; rep from * to end.

Row 5 Knit.

Change to larger needles.

Work in garter st until desired length.

Bind off very loosely.

(Extra fullness can be added by repeating row 4 once more after working row 5 and then continuing on larger needles for the desired length.

peasant ruffle

▲ (Cast on double the amount of sts needed—beg with a multiple of 4 sts plus 2 and end with a multiple of 2 sts plus 1)

Row 1 (RS) K1, *SKP, yo twice, k2tog; rep from *, end k1.

Row 2 P1, *p1, (p1, k1) in yo, p1; rep from *, end p1.

Rep rows 1 and 2 until desired length.

Next (dec) row K2tog across.

Cont as desired.

angled ruffle

▼ With A, cast on sts needed for project.

Work in desired pat. Change to B.

Next (inc) row (RS) Inc 1 in each st across.

Work in St st for 1"/2.5cm.

Bind off 3 sts at beg of next 6 rows. (**Note** 1 or 2 sts may be bound off for a different degree of the angle.)

Next row (RS) Bind off rem sts.

two textured gathered ruffle

▼ (multiple of 2 sts plus 1)

• Use 2 different size needles and 2 different yarns

With smaller needles and A, work 8 rows (or desired length) in k1, p1 rib.

Change to larger needles and B.

Next (inc) row (RS) K1, inc 1 in each st across.

Work in St st until desired length.

Bind off.

1 x 1 wide rib ruffle

▼ (over an odd number of sts) ▶◀

• You can eliminate the ribbing and just work rows 1 to 10.

• You can add a contrasting edge by binding off using a contrasting color.

Work in k1, p1 rib for ½"/1.25cm, end with a WS row.

Row 1 (RS) K1, *p1, M1 p-st, k1; rep from * to end.

Row 2 and all WS rows K the knit sts and p the purl sts.

Row 3 K1, *p2, M1 p-st, k1; rep from * to end.

Row 5 K1, *p3, M1 p-st, k1; rep from * to end.

Row 7 K1, *p4, M1 p-st, k1; rep from * to end.

Row 9 K1, *p5, M1 p-st, k1; rep from * to end.

Row 10 Rep row 2.

Bind off knitwise.

rib ruffle combo

▲ (Cast on double the amount of sts needed, plus 5–beg with a multiple of 20 sts plus 5 and end with a multiple of 10 sts plus 5)

Row 1 (WS) *[P1, k1] twice, p1, k15; rep from *, end [p1, k1] twice, p1.

Row 2 *[K1, p1] twice, k1, p15; rep from *, end [k1, p1] twice, k1.

Rep rows 1 and 2 until desired length, end with a RS row.

Next (dec) row 1 (WS) *[P1, k1] twice, p1, [k3tog] 5 times; rep from *, end [p1, k1] twice, p1.

Next row K1, *p1, k1; rep from * to end.

Cont as desired.

seed stitch ruffle A

▲ (Cast on twice the number of sts needed plus 1-for an odd number of sts)
Row 1 K1, *p1, k1; rep from * to end.
Row 2 K the purl sts and p the knit sts.
Rep row 2 until desired length.
Next (dec) row (RS) K1, k2tog across.
Cont as desired.

seed stitch ruffle B

▲ (Cast on twice the number of sts needed for an even number of sts)
Row 1 *K1, p1; rep from * to end.
Row 2 K the purl sts and p the knit sts.
Rep row 2 until desired length.
Next (dec) row (RS) K2tog across.
Cont as desired.

bobble ruffle

▲ (Cast on 3 times the number of sts needed that is a multiple of 8 sts plus 7)
MB—Make Bobble
K into front, back, front, back and front of next st—5 sts, turn, p5 turn, k5, pass 2nd, 3rd, 4th and 5th sts over first st.
Row 1 (RS) *K7, MB; rep from *, end k7.
Next row Purl.
Cont in St st until desired length, end with a WS row.
Next (dec) row *K1, k3tog; rep from *, end k3.
Cont in k1, p1 rib until desired length.

lift lace ruffle

▲ (Cast on 3 times the number of sts needed that is a multiple of 3 sts)
Set up row K2, *yo, k1; rep from * to end. P 1 row.
Row 1 (RS) K2, *yo, k3, lift first st of these 3 sts over 2nd and 3rd st; rep from *, end k1.
Row 2 and all WS rows Purl.
Row 3 K1, *k3, lift first st of these 3 sts over 2nd and 3rd st, yo; rep from *, end k2.
Row 4 Purl.
Rep rows 1 to 4 twice more, then rep rows 1 and 2 once more.
Next (dec) row K2, *k3tog tbl; rep from *, end k1.
Next row Purl.
Cont as desired.

baby cable ruffle

▲ (Cast on twice the number of sts needed that is a multiple of 4 sts plus 2)

Row 1 (RS) P2, *k2, p2; rep from * to end.

Row 2 K2, *p2, k2; rep from * to end.

Row 3 P2, *RT, p2; rep from * to end.

Row 4 Rep row 2.

Rep rows 1 to 4 for 2"/5cm or desired length, end with a WS row.

Next (dec) row (RS) P2tog, *k2tog, p2tog; rep from * to end.

Cont as desired.

feather lace ruffle

▲ (Cast on 3 times the number of sts needed that is a multiple of 9 sts plus 4)

Rows 1, 2 and 3 Knit.

Rows 4, 6 and 8 Purl.

Row 5 (RS) K3, *yo, k2, ssk, k2tog, k2, yo, k1; rep from *, end last rep k2.

Row 7 K2, *yo, k2, ssk, k2tog, k2, yo, k1; rep from *, end last rep k3.

Rep rows 5 to 8 once more.

Next (dec) row (RS) K1, k3tog across.

Cont as desired.

eyelet point ruffle

▲ (Cast on 3 times the number of sts needed that is a multiple of 14 sts plus 1)

Row 1 and all WS rows Purl.

Rows 2, 4, 6, 8, 10 and 12 K1, *yo, k3, SKP, yo, SK2P, yo, k2tog, k3, yo, k1; rep from * to end.

Row 14 (RS) K3tog across.

Note If there are not enough sts at end of rep to work k3tog, then work k2tog, or k1.

Cont as desired.

gazebo lace ruffle

▲ (Cast on 3 times the number of sts needed that is a multiple of 10 sts plus 1)

Make Bobble (MB)

[P1, k1, p1] in next st, turn, k3, turn, p3, turn, k3, pass 2nd and 3rd st over first st.

Set-up row (WS) P5, *MB, p4; rep from *, end last rep p5.

Row 1 (RS) K1, *yo, k3, SK2P, k3, yo, k1; rep from * to end.

Row 2 Purl.

Row 3 P1, *k1, yo, k2, SK2P, k2, yo, k1, p1; rep from * to end.

Rows 4 and 6 *K1, p9; rep from *, end k1.

Row 5 P1, *k2, yo, k1, SK2P, k1, yo, k2, p1; rep from * to end.

Row 7 P1, *k3, yo, SK2P, yo, k3, p1; rep from * to end.

Row 8 Purl.

Row 9 K1, *k3, yo, SK2P, yo, k4; rep from * to end.

Rep rows 8 and 9 for 1"/2.5cm or desired length, end with a WS row.

Next (dec) row K1, work k3tog across.

Note If there are not enough sts at end of rep to work k3tog, then work k2tog, or k1.

Cont as desired.

sawtooth lace ruffle

▶ Cast on 16 sts.

Row 1 K10, [yo, k2tog] twice, yo, k2.

Row 2 K9, p5, w & t.

Row 3 K8, [yo, k2tog] twice, yo, k2.

Row 4 K10, p5, k3.

Row 5 K12, [yo, k2tog] twice, yo, k2.

Row 6 K11, p5, w & t.

Row 7 P5, k5, [yo, k2tog] twice, yo, k2.

Row 8 K20.

Row 9 K3, p5, k6, [yo, k2tog] twice, yo, k2.

Row 10 K18, w & t.

Row 11 P5, k13.

Row 12 Bind off 5 sts, k to end.

Rep rows 1 to 12 until desired length. Bind off.

spoke picot combo

Work **picot hem** (see page 147) then work **spoke point ruffle** (see page 60).

basic ruffle with picot hem

▲ (Cast on 3 times the number of sts needed that is a multiple of 2 sts plus 1)

Work in St st for ½"/1.25cm, end with a WS row.

Picot row (RS) K1, *yo, k2tog; rep from * to end.

Beg with a p row and cont in St st or desired pat until desired length, end with a WS row.

Next (dec) row K3tog across, end k1.

Fold hem at picot row and sew in place, then cont as desired.

spiral ruffle

▼ (multiple of 4 sts)

Row 1 (RS) *K4, yo; rep from *, end k4.

Row 2 and WS rows Purl.

Row 3 *K5, yo; rep from *, end k4.

Row 4 Purl.

Cont as established, working incs on every RS row, and working 1 st more in each rep, until desired length. Bind off.

peplum ruffle

▼ (multiple of 5 sts plus 4)

Row 1 (RS) K3 *inc1 twice, k3; rep from *, end last rep k4.

Row 2 and all WS rows Purl.

Row 3 K4 *inc1 twice, k5; rep from *, end last rep k5.

Row 5 K5, *inc1 twice, k7; rep from *, end last rep k6.

Row 7 K6, *inc1 twice, k9; rep from *, end last rep k7.

Row 9 K7, *inc1 twice, k11; rep from *, end last rep k8.

Cont as established, working incs on every RS row, and working 2 sts more in each rep, until desired length. Bind off.

spoke point ruffle

▲ (beg with a multiple of 14 sts plus 11 and end with a
multiple of 4 sts plus 3)

Row 1 (RS) Knit.

Row 2 and all WS rows Purl.

Row 3 K11, *DD, k11; rep from * to end.

Row 5 K10, *DD, k9; rep from *, end last rep k10.

Row 7 K9, *DD, k7; rep from *, end last rep k9.

Row 9 K8, *DD, k5; rep from *, end last rep k8.

Row 11 K7, *DD, k3; rep from *, end last rep k7.

Cont as desired.

knitted fluted edge or border

▼ (begin with a multiple of 6 sts plus 2)

Rows 1, 3 and 5 P2 *k4, p2; rep from * to end.

Rows 2, 4 and 6 K2, *p4, k2; rep from * to end.

Row 7 P2, *k2, yo, k2, p2; rep from * to end.

Row 8 K2, *p5, k2; rep from * to end.

Row 9 P2, *k2, yo, k1, yo, k2, p2; rep from * to end.

Row 10 K2, *p7, k2; rep from * to end.

Row 11 P2, *k2, yo, k3, yo, k2, p2; rep from * to end.

Row 12 K2, *p9, k2; rep from * to end.

Row 13 P2, *k2, yo, k5, yo, k2, p2; rep from * to end.

Row 14 K2, *p11, k2; rep from * to end.

Row 15 P2, *k2, yo, k7, yo, k2, p2; rep from * to end.

Row 16 K2, *p13, k2; rep from * to end.

Row 17 P2, *k2, yo, k9, yo, k2, p2; rep from * to end.

Row 18 K2, *p15, k2; rep from * to end.

Row 19 P2, *k2, yo, k11, yo, k2, p2; rep from * to end.

Row 20 K2, *p17, k2; rep from * to end.

Row 21 P2, *k2, yo, k13, yo, k2, p2; rep from * to end.

Bind off.

ruffle rib scallop

▲ (beg with a multiple of 20 sts plus 9 and end with a multiple of 8 sts plus 1)

Rows 1, 3, 5 and 7 (RS) K1, *p1, k1; rep from * to end.

Row 2 Purl.

Row 4 (WS) P5, k3tog, *p13, k3tog, p1, k3tog; rep from *, end last rep, p13, k3tog, p5.

Row 6 P5, k3tog, *p9, k3tog, p1, k3tog; rep from *, end last rep, p9, k3tog, p5.

Row 8 P5, k3tog, *p5, k3tog, p1, k3tog; rep from *, end last rep, p5, k3tog, p5.

Cont in established rib or k1, p1 rib as desired.

short rib ruffle

▲ (Cast on 3 times the number of sts needed that is a multiple of 3 sts)

Work St st for 1"/2.5cm, end with a WS row.

Next (dec) row (RS) K3tog across.

Next row *K1, p1; rep from * to end.

Cont in k1, p1 rib or as desired.

three-way fru fru ruffle

▼ (any number of sts)

P 1 row, k 1 row, p 1 row.

Next (inc) row (RS) Inc 1 in each st across.

Beg with a WS row and cont in St st until desired length.

Bind off.

gossamer ruffle

 (beg with a multiple of 3 sts plus 1 and end with a multiple of 2 sts plus 1)

• Cast on using Double Cast-On Method.

• Dropping a stitch makes the lacy effect.

Row 1 (RS) K1 tbl, *p2, k1 tbl; rep from * to end.

Row 2 P1, *k1 tbl, k1, p1; rep from * to end.

Rows 3, 5, 7, 9 and 11 Rep row 1.

Rows 4, 6, 8, 10 and 12 Rep row 2.

Row 13 K1 tbl, *sl next st off needle and allow it to drop to cast-on edge, p1, k1 tbl; rep from * to end.

Row 14 P1, *k1 tbl, p1; rep from * to end.

Row 15 K1 tbl, *p1, k1 tbl; rep from * to end.

Rows 16 and 18 Rep row 14.

Rows 17 and 19 Rep row 15.

Cont as desired.

sawtooth antique

▶ Cast on 5 sts.

Row 1 (RS) Sl 1, yo, k2tog, yo, k2.

Row 2 and all WS rows Sl 1, k to end.

Row 3 Sl 1, [yo, k2tog] twice, yo, k1.

Row 5 Sl 1, [yo, k2tog] twice, yo, k2.

Row 7 Sl 1, [yo, k2tog] 3 times, yo, k1.

Row 9 Sl 1, [yo, k2tog] 3 times, yo, k2.

Row 11 Sl 1, [yo, k2tog] 4 times, yo, k1.

Row 13 Sl 1, [yo, k2tog] 4 times, yo, k2.

Row 15 Bind off 8 sts, yo, k2tog, yo, k1.

Row 16 Rep row 2.

Rep rows 1 to 16 until desired length. Bind off.

lace bells

▲ (beg with a multiple of 14 sts plus 3
and end with a multiple of 4 sts plus 3)

Rows 1 and 2 Knit.

Row 3 (RS) P3, *k11, p3; rep from * to end.

Row 4 K3, *p11, k3; rep from * to end.

Row 5 P3, *SKP, k2, yo, SK2P, yo, k2,
k2tog, p3; rep from * to end.

Row 6 K3, *p9, k3; rep from * to end.

Row 7 P3, *SKP, k1, yo, SK2P, yo, k1,
k2tog, p3; rep from * to end.

Row 8 K3, *p7, k3; rep from * to end.

Row 9 P3, *SKP, yo, SK2P, yo, k2tog, p3;
rep from * to end.

Row 10 K3, *p5, k3; rep from * to end.

Row 11 P3, *SKP, k1, k2tog, p3; rep from *
to end.

Row 12 K3, *p3, k3; rep from * to end.

Row 13 P3, *SK2P, p3; rep from * to end.

Row 14 K3, *p1, k3; rep from * to end.

Row 15 P3, *k1, p3; rep from * to end.

Row 16 Rep row 14.

Rep rows 15 and 16 for p3, k1 rib as
established or as desired.

belle epoque

▼ (begin with a multiple of 8 sts plus 7)

• This ruffle looks most attractive when bound-
off with a picot edge.

Row 1 (RS) P7, *k1, p7; rep from * across.

Row 2 K7, *p1, k7; rep from * across.

Row 3 P7, *yo, k1, yfrn, p7; rep from * to end.

Row 4 K7, *p2, p1 tbl, k7; rep from * to end.

Row 5 P7, *yo, k3, yfrn, p7; rep from * to end.

Row 6 K7, *p4, p1 tbl, k7; rep from * to end.

Row 7 P7, *yo, k5, yfrn, p7; rep from * to end.

Row 8 K7, *p6, p1 tbl, k7; rep from * to end.

Row 9 P7, *yo, k7, yfrn, p7; rep from * to end.

Row 10 K7, *p8, p1 tbl, k7; rep from * to end.

Row 11 P7, *yo, k9, yfrn, p7; rep from * to end.

Row 12 K7, *p10, p1 tbl, k7; rep from * to end.

Row 13 P7, *yo, k11, yfrn, p7; rep from * to end.

Row 14 K7, *p12, p1 tbl, k7; rep from * to end.

Row 15 P7, *yo, k13, yfrn, p7; rep from * to end.

Row 16 K7, *p14, p1 tbl, k7; rep from * to end.

Bind off with a picot edge as foll: Bind off 2 sts,
*sl st back to LH needle, using the cable cast-on
method, cast on 3 sts, then bind off 5 sts; rep
from * to end.

Fasten off.

ruffles

reversed kick pleat

▲ (Beg with a multiple of 7 sts plus 4 and end with a multiple of 5 sts plus 4 sts) ◄►

Rows 1 and 3 (WS) *K4, p3; rep from *, end k4.

Rows 2, 4, 6, 8, 10 and 12 K the knit sts and p the purl sts.

Row 5 *K4, p2tog, p1; rep from *, end k4.

Row 7 *K4, p2; rep from *, end k4.

Row 9 *K4, p2tog; rep from *, end k4.

Row 11 *K4, p1; rep from *, end k4.

Row 13 *K4, k2tog; rep from *, end k4.

Row 14 Purl.

Cont as desired.

bold bell ruffle

▼ (begin with multiple of 8 sts plus 7) ◄►

Row 1 (RS) P7, *k1, p7; rep from * to end.

Row 2 K7, *p1, k7; rep from * to end.

Row 3 P7, *yo, k1, yfrn, p7; rep from * to end.

Row 4 K7, *p2, p1 tbl, k7; rep from * to end.

Row 5 P7, *yo, k3, yfrn, p7; rep from * to end.

Row 6 K7, *p4, p1 tbl, k7; rep from * to end.

Row 7 P7, *yo, k5, yfrn, p7; rep from * to end.

Row 8 K7, *p6, p1 tbl, k7; rep from * to end.

Row 9 P7, *yo, k7, yfrn, p7; rep from * to end.

Row 10 K7, *p8, p1 tbl, k7; rep from * to end.

Row 11 P7, *yo, k9, yfrn, p7; rep from * to end.

Row 12 K7, *p10, p1 tbl, k7; rep from * to end.

Row 13 P7, *yo, k11, yfrn, p7; rep from * to end.

Row 14 K7, *p12, p1 tbl, k7; rep from * to end.

Bind off.

double petite bell ruffle

▲ Bottom layer

Work as for Petite Bell Ruffle until piece measures 3"/7.5cm from beg. Place sts on a spare needle.

Top layer

Work as for Petite Bell Ruffle until piece measures 2"/5cm from beg.

Join layers

Work sts of both layers tog, using 3-needle joining technique.

Cont in pat or as desired.

petite bell ruffle

▲ (beg with a multiple of 12 sts plus 3 and end with a multiple of 4 sts plus 3) ◄►

Row 1 (RS) P3, *k9, p3; rep from * to end.

Row 2 K3, *p9, k3; rep from * to end.

Row 3 P3, *SKP, k5, k2tog, p3; rep from * to end.

Row 4 K3, *p7, k3; rep from * to end.

Row 5 P3, *SKP, k3, k2tog, p3; rep from * to end.

Row 6 K3, *p5, k3; rep from * to end.

Row 7 P3, *SKP, k1, k2tog, p3; rep from * to end.

Row 8 K3, *p3, k3; rep from * to end.

Row 9 P3, *SK2P, p3; rep from * to end.

Row 10 K3, *p1, k3; rep from * to end.

Row 11 P3, *k1, p3; rep from * to end.

Row 12 Rep row 10.

Cont to rep rows 11 and 12 for p3, k1 rib or as desired.

kick pleat

▲ (Beg with a multiple of 7 sts plus 4 and end with a multiple of 5 sts plus 4) ◄►

Rows 1 and 3 (RS) *K4, p3; rep from *, end k4.

Rows 2, 4, 6, 8, 10 and 12 K the knit sts and p the purl sts.

Row 5 *K4, p2tog, p1; rep from *, end k4.

Row 7 *K4, p2; rep from *, end k4.

Row 9 *K4, p2tog; rep from *, end k4.

Row 11 *K4, p1; rep from *, end k4.

Row 13 *K4, k2tog; rep from *, end k4.

Row 14 Purl.

Cont as desired.

reversed bold bell ruffle

▼ (multiple of 8 sts plus 7) ◄►

Row 1 (WS) P7, *k1, p7; rep from * to end.

Row 2 K7, *p1, k7; rep from * to end.

Row 3 P7, *yo, k1, yfrn, p7; rep from * to end.

Row 4 K7, *p2, p1 tbl, k7; rep from * to end.

Row 5 P7, *yo, k3, yfrn, p7; rep from * to end.

Row 6 K7, *p4, p1 tbl, k7; rep from * to end.

Row 7 P7, *yo, k5, yfrn, p7; rep from * to end.

Row 8 K7, *p6, p1 tbl, k7; rep from * to end.

Row 9 P7, *yo, k7, yfrn, p7; rep from * to end.

Row 10 K7, *p8, p1 tbl, k7; rep from * to end.

Row 11 P7, *yo, k9, yfrn, p7; rep from * to end.

Row 12 K7, *p10, p1 tbl, k7; rep from * to end.

Row 13 P7, *yo, k11, yfrn, p7; rep from * to end.

Row 14 K7, *p12, p1 tbl, k7; rep from * to end.

Bind off.

reversed petite bell ruffle

▲ (beg with a multiple of 12 sts plus 3 and end with a multiple of 4 sts plus 3) ◄►

Row 1 (WS) P3, *k9, p3; rep from * to end.

Row 2 K3, *p9, k3; rep from * to end.

Row 3 P3, *SKP, k5, k2tog, p3; rep from * to end.

Row 4 K3, *p7, k3; rep from * to end.

Row 5 P3, *SKP, k3, k2tog, p3; rep from * to end.

Row 6 K3, *p5, k3; rep from * to end.

Row 7 P3, *SKP, k1, k2tog, p3; rep from * to end.

Row 8 K3, *p3, k3; rep from * to end.

Row 9 P3, *SK2P, p3; rep from * to end.

Row 10 K3, *p1, k3; rep from * to end.

Row 11 P3, *k1, p3; rep from * to end.

Row 12 Rep row 10.

Cont to rep rows 11 and 12 for k3, p1 rib or as desired.

mock pleat

▲ (Cast on twice the number of sts needed that is a multiple of 8 sts)

Row 1 (RS) *K7, p1; rep from * to end.

Row 2 K4, *p1, k7; rep from * to last 4 sts, p1, k3.

Rep these 2 rows until desired length, end with a WS row.

Next (dec) row (RS) K2tog across.

Cont as desired.

vertical pleat

▶ Cast on 15 sts. ◀▶

Row 1 Knit.

Row 2 P12, w & t, k12.

Row 3 P12, k3.

Row 4 K3, p12.

Row 5 K12, w & t, p12.

Row 6 Knit.

Rep rows 1 to 6 until desired length. Bind off.

• The length of this ruffle can be made longer
or shorter by casting on more or less sts.

triangle on pleats

▲ (multiple of 10 sts) ◀▶

Rows 1 and 8 *P2, k8; rep from * to end.

Rows 2 and 9 *P7, k3; rep from * to end.

Rows 3 and 10 *P4, k6; rep from * to end.

Rows 4 and 11 *P5, k5; rep from * to end.

Rows 5 and 12 *P6, k4; rep from * to end.

Rows 6 and 13 *P3, k7; rep from * to end.

Rows 7 and 14 *P8, k2; rep from * to end.

Rep rows 1 to 14 until desired length of ruffle.

Cont as desired.

smocked ruffle

▲ (multiple of 4 sts plus 3)

Row 1 (RS) P3, *k1, p3; rep from * to end.

Row 2 K3, *p1, k3; rep from * to end.

Rep rows 1 and 2 until piece measures 1¼"/3cm or desired length.

Smocked row 1 (RS) *Rib 8 sts, sl last 5 sts on RH needle to cn and hold to front, wrap yarn clockwise twice around these sts, end wyib, sl these 5 sts to RH needle; rep from * to end.

Work 3 rows in p3, k1 rib.

Smocked row 2 Rib 12 sts, *sl last 5 sts on RH needle to cn and hold to front, wrap yarn clockwise twice around these sts, end wyib, sl these 5 sts to RH needle, rib 8 sts; rep from * to end.

Work 3 rows in p3, k1 rib.

Cont as desired.

slip stitch variation smocking

▲ (multiple of 6 sts plus 2)

Row 1 (RS) *P2, k4; rep from *, end p2.

Rows 2 and 4 *K2, p4; rep from *, end k2.

Row 3 *P2, insert RH needle between 4th and 5th sts and draw through a loop, k4, then sl loop over the 4 sts; rep from *, end p2.

Row 5 K3, p2, *k4, p2; rep from *, end k3.

Row 6 P3, k2, *p4, k2; rep from *, end p3.

Row 7 K1, insert RH needle between 4th and 5th sts and draw through a loop, k4, then sl loop over the 4 sts, *p2, insert RH needle between 4th and 5th sts and draw through a lp, k4, then sl lp over the 4 sts; rep from *, end p2, insert RH needle between 4th and 5th sts and draw through a lp, k4, then sl lp over the 2 sts, k1.

Row 8 Rep row 6.

Rep rows 1 to 8 once.

Cont in p2, k4 rib or as desired.

2 X 2 rib smocking

▲ (multiple of 8 sts plus 2)

Prep Row (RS) P2, *k2, p2; rep from * to end.

Rows 1 and 3 K2, *p2, k2; rep from * to end.

Row 2 P2, *k2, p2; rep from * to end.

Row 4 P2, *insert RH needle between 6th and 7th sts and draw through a loop, sl loop to LH needle and k it tog with first st on LH needle, k1, p2, k2, p2: rep from * to end.

Rows 5 and 7 Rep row 1.

Row 6 Rep row 2.

Row 8 P2, k2, p2, *insert RH needle between 6th and 7th sts and draw through a lp, sl lp to LH needle and k it tog with first st on LH needle, k1, p2, k2, p2: rep from *, end k2, p2.

Rep rows 1 to 8 once.

Cont in k2, p2 rib or as desired.

lace

filet picot

▶ Cast on 7 sts.

Rows 1, 3, 5 and 7 Knit.

Row 2 K2, [yo, k2tog] twice, yo, k1.

Row 4 K2, [yo, k2tog] twice, yo, k2.

Row 6 K2, [yo, k2tog] 3 times, yo, k1.

Row 8 K2, [yo, k2tog] 3 times, yo, k2.

Row 9 Bind off 4 sts, k6.

Rep rows 2 to 9 until desired length.

Bind off.

Multiple Yarn Overs

When working lace patterns, the yarn over is one of the most important elements. Normally one yarn over is worked to compensate for a decrease. On the following row, you work the yarn over as a stitch. There are some cases where two or more yarn overs are worked. Sometimes these yarn overs are dropped on the

baby tears

▶ Cast on 7 sts.

Row 1 K3, yo, k2tog, yo twice, k2.

Row 2 K3, p1, k2, yo, k2tog, k1.

Row 3 K3, yo, k2tog, k4.

Row 4 Bind off 2 sts, k3, yo, k2tog, k1.

Rep rows 1 to 4 until desired length.

Bind off.

eyelet points

▶ Cast on 5 sts.

Row 1 Sl 1, k1, yo twice, k2tog, k1.

Row 2 Sl 1, k2, p1, k2.

Row 3 Sl 1, k3, yo twice, k2.

Row 4 Sl 1, k2, p1, k4.

Row 5 Sl 1, k1, yo twice, k2tog, k4.

Row 6 Sl 1, k5, p1, k2.

Row 7 Sl 1, k8.

Row 8 Bind off 4 sts, k4.

Rep rows 1 to 8 until desired length.

Bind off.

next row to create elongated stitches which is stated in the instructions. If the extra yarn overs are not dropped, then each yarn over is considered one stitch. For example, if you work a double yarn over on one row, then you must work two stitches (1 in each yarn over loop) on the following row.

cyprus

▶ Cast on 8 sts.

P2tog

P the next st tog with the first yo, dropping the 2nd yo. K 1 row.

Row 1 Sl 1, k1, yo twice, p2tog, k2, yo 3 times, k2.

Row 2 K2, k1, p1, k1, k2, yo twice, p2tog, k2.

Row 3 Sl 1, k1, yo twice, p2tog, k7.

Row 4 K7, yo twice, p2tog, k2.

Row 5 Sl 1, k1, yo twice, p2tog, k7.

Row 6 Bind off 3 sts, k3, yo twice, p2tog, k2.

Rep rows 1 to 6 until desired length.

Bind off.

petite open points

▶ Cast on 8 sts

Row 1 Knit.

Row 2 Sl 1, k2, yo, k2tog, k1, yo 4 times, k2.

Row 3 Sl 1, k1, [k1, p1] twice into the yo 4 times, k3, yo, k2tog, k1.

Row 4 Sl 1, k2, yo, k2tog, k7.

Row 5 Sl 1, k8, yo, k2tog, k1.

Row 6 Sl 1, k2, yo, k2tog, k7.

Row 7 Bind off 4 sts, k4, yo, k2tog, k1.

Rep rows 2 to 7 until desired length.

Bind off.

eyelet kiss

▶ Cast on 12 sts.

Row 1 Sl 1, k5, k2tog, yo, k1, k2tog, k1.

Row 2 K4, yo, k2tog, k2, yo, k2tog, k1.

Row 3 Sl 1, k3, k2tog, yo, k1, k2tog, k2.

Row 4 K7, yo, k2tog, k1.

Row 5 Sl 1, k4, yo, k2tog, k1, yo twice, k2.

Row 6 K3, p1, k2, yo, k3, yo, k2tog, k1.

Row 7 Sl 1, k6, yo, k2tog, k4.

Row 8 Bind off 2 sts, k2, yo, k5, yo, k2tog, k1.

Rep rows 1 to 8 until desired length.

Bind off.

slant eyelet

▶ Cast on 8 sts.

Prep row Knit.

Row 1 Sl 1, k1, [yo, k2tog] twice, yo, k2.

Rows 2, 4, 6 and 8 Sl 1, k to end.

Row 3 Sl 1, k2, [yo, k2tog] twice, yo, k2.

Row 5 Sl 1, k3, [yo, k2tog] twice, yo, k2.

Row 7 Sl 1, k4, [yo, k2tog] twice, yo, k2.

Row 9 Sl 1, k11.

Row 10 Bind off 4 sts, k7.

Rep rows 1 to 10 until desired length.

Bind off.

shark's tooth

▶ Cast on 8 sts.

Row 1 Knit.

Row 2 Sl 1, k2, yo, k2tog, yo, SKP, k1.

Row 3 Sl 1, p1, [k1, p1] in yo, k2, yo, k2tog, k1.

Row 4 Sl 1, k2, yo, k2tog, k1, yo, SKP, k1.

Row 5 Sl 1, p1, [k1, p1] in yo, p1, k2, yo, k2tog, k1.

Row 6 Sl 1, k2, yo, k2tog, k2, yo, SKP, k1.

Row 7 Sl 1, p1, [k1, p1] in yo, p2, k2, yo, k2tog, k1.

Row 8 Sl 1, k2, yo, k2tog, k3, yo, SKP, k1.

Row 9 Sl 1, p1, [k1, p1] in yo, p3, k2, yo, k2tog, k1.

Row 10 Sl 1, k2, yo, k2tog, k1, yo, k2tog, k1, yo, SKP, k1.

Row 11 Sl 1, p1, [k1, p1] in yo, p4, k2, yo, k2tog, k1.

Row 12 Sl 1, k2, yo, k2tog, k8.

Row 13 Bind off 5 sts, p2, k2, yo, k2tog, k1.

Rep rows 2 to 13 until desired length.

Bind off.

chevron lattice

▶ Cast on 15 sts.

Row 1 (RS) Sl 1, k4, [yo, k2tog] 4 times, yo, k2.

Row 2 and all WS rows Knit.

Row 3 Sl 1, k5, [yo, k2tog] 4 times, yo, k2.

Row 5 Sl 1, k6, [yo, k2tog] 4 times, yo, k2.

Row 7 Sl 1, k7, [yo, k2tog] 4 times, yo, k2.

Row 9 Sl 1, k5, k2tog, [yo, k2tog] 5 times, k1.

Row 11 Sl 1, k4, k2tog, [yo, k2tog] 5 times, k1.

Row 13 Sl 1, k3, k2tog, [yo, k2tog] 5 times, k1.

Row 15 Sl 1, k2, k2tog, [yo, k2tog] 5 times, k1.

Row 16 Knit.

Rep rows 1 to 16 until desired length.

Bind off.

molly's lace

▶ Cast on 9 sts.

Row 1 Sl 1, k1, yo, k2tog, [yo, k1] 3 times, yo, k2.

Row 2 P11, k2.

Row 3 Sl 1, k1, yo, k2tog, yo, k3, yo, k1, yo, k3, yo, k2.

Row 4 P15, k2.

Row 5 Sl 1, k1, yo, k2tog, yo, (sl 2, k3tog, psso), yo, k1, yo, (sl 2, k3tog, psso), yo, k2.

Row 6 Bind off 4 sts, p6, k2.

Rep rows 1 to 6 until desired length.

Bind off.

scalloped trellis

▶ Cast on 13 sts.

Row 1 and all RS rows K2, p to last 2 sts, k2.

Row 2 K7, yo, SKP, yo, k4.

Row 4 K6, [yo, SKP] twice, yo, k4.

Row 6 K5, [yo, SKP] 3 times, yo, k4.

Row 8 K4, [yo, SKP] 4 times, yo, k4.

Row 10 K3, [yo, SKP] 5 times, yo, k4.

Row 12 K4, [yo, SKP] 5 times, k2tog, k2.

Row 14 K5, [yo, SKP] 4 times, k2tog, k2.

Row 16 K6, [yo, SKP] 3 times, k2tog, k2.

Row 18 K7, [yo SKP] twice, k2tog, k2.

Row 20 K8, yo, SKP, k2tog, k2.

Rep rows 1 to 20 until desired length.

Bind off.

small duster scallop

▶ Cast on 13 sts.

Row 1 Sl 1, k1, yo, k2tog, k5, yo, k2tog, yo, k2.

Row 2 and all even rows Yo, k2tog, k to end.

Row 3 Sl 1, k1, yo, k2tog, k4, [yo, k2tog] twice, yo, k2.

Row 5 Sl 1, k1, yo, k2tog, k3, [yo, k2tog] 3 times, yo, k2.

Row 7 Sl 1, k1, yo, k2tog, k2, [yo, k2tog] 4 times, yo, k2.

Row 9 Sl 1, k1, yo, k2tog, k1, [yo, k2tog] 5 times, yo, k2.

Row 11 Sl 1, k1, yo, k2tog, k1, k2tog, [yo, k2tog] 5 times, k1.

Row 13 Sl 1, k1, yo, k2tog, k2, k2tog, [yo, k2tog] 4 times, k1.

Row 15 Sl 1, k1, yo, k2tog, k3, k2tog, [yo, k2tog] 3 times, k1.

Row 17 Sl 1, k1, yo, k2tog, k4, k2tog, [yo, k2tog] twice, k1.

Row 19 Sl 1, k1, yo, k2tog, k5, k2tog, yo, k2tog, k1.

Row 20 Yo, k2tog, k11.

Rep rows 1 to 20 until desired length.

Bind off.

merry-go-rounds

▶ Cast on 23 sts.

K 1 row.

Row 1 K2, yo, k5, yo, k2tog, k1, k2tog, yo, k11.

Row 2 K2, yo, k1, SK2P, k1, yo, k17.

Row 3 K2, yo, k1, k2tog, yo twice, SK2P, k1, yo, SK2P, yo, k12.

Row 4 K2, yo, k1, SK2P, k1, yo, k10, [k1, p1, k1 into yo twice], k5.

Row 5 K1, k2tog, yo, k2tog, k3, k2tog, yo, k3, yo, k2tog, k10.

Row 6 K2, yo, k1, SK2P, k1, yo, k17.

Row 7 K1, k2tog, yo, k2tog, k1, k2tog, yo, k5, yo, k2tog, k9.

Row 8 K2, yo, k1, SK2P, k1, yo, k16.

Row 9 K1, k2tog, yo, SK2P, yo, k1, k2tog, yo twice, SK2P, k1, yo, k2tog, k8.

Row 10 K2, yo, k1, SK2P, k1, yo, k5, [k1, p1, k1 into yo twice], k7.

Row 11 K2, yo, k3, yo, k2tog, k3, k2tog, yo, k10.

Row 12 K2, yo, k1, SK2P, k1, yo, k16.

Rep rows 1 to 12 until desired length.

Bind off.

diamond lattice

▶ Cast on 22 sts.

Row 1 (RS) K5, [k2tog, yo, k4] twice, k2tog, yo, k3tog.

Row 2 Yo, k20.

Row 3 K4, [k2tog, yo, k1, yo, k2tog, k1] twice, k2tog, yo, k1, yo, k2tog.

Row 4 Yo, k21.

Row 5 K3, k2tog, yo, [k3, yo, k3tog, yo] twice, k3, yo, k2tog.

Row 6 Yo, k22.

Row 7 K2, [k2tog, yo, k4] twice, k2tog, yo, k5, yo, k2tog.

Row 8 Yo, k23.

Row 9 K4, [yo, k2tog, k1, k2tog, yo, k1] twice, yo, k2tog, k1, k2tog, yo, k3tog.

Row 10 Yo, k22.

Row 11 K5, [yo, k3tog, yo, k3] twice, [yo, k3tog] twice.

Row 12 Yo, k21.

Rep rows 1 to 12 until desired length.

Bind off.

spider web

▶ Cast on 15 sts.
K 1 row.

Row 1 K3, yo, k3tog, yo, k3, yo, k2tog, [yo twice, k2tog] twice.

Row 2 Yo, [k2, p1] twice, k2, yo, k2tog, k7.

Row 3 K3, [yo, k2tog] twice, p1, k2tog, yo, k8.

Row 4 K1, bind off 3 sts, k3, p6, k1, yo, k2tog, k1.

Row 5 K3, yo, k2tog, k1, yo, k3tog, yo, k2, [yo twice, k2tog] twice.

Row 6 Yo, [k2, p1] twice, k1, p6, k1, yo, k2tog, k1.

Row 7 K3, yo, k2tog twice, yo, k1, yo, k2tog, k8.

Row 8 K1, bind off 3 sts, k3, p6, k1, yo, k2tog, k1.

Rep rows 1 to 8 until desired length. Bind off.

irish lace

▶ Cast on 20 sts.

Row 1 Sl 1, k1, [yo, k2tog] 4 times, k3, k2tog, yo, k3, yo, k2.

Row 2 Yo, k2tog, k19.

Row 3 Sl 1, k2, [yo, k2tog] 3 times, k3, k2tog, yo, k5, yo, k2.

Row 4 Yo, k2tog, k20.

Row 5 Sl 1, k1, [yo, k2tog] 3 times, k3, k2tog, yo, k2tog twice, yo 3 times, k2tog, k1, yo, k2.

Row 6 Yo, k2tog, k4, p1, k1, p1, k14.

Row 7 Sl 1, k2, [yo, k2tog] 3 times, k4, yo, k2tog, k3, k2tog, yo, k2tog, k1.

Row 8 Yo, k2tog, k20.

Row 9 Sl 1, k1, [yo, k2tog] 4 times, k4, yo, k2tog, k1, k2tog, yo, k2tog, k1.

Row 10 Yo, k2tog, k19.

Row 11 Sl 1, k2, [yo, k2tog] 4 times, k4, yo, k3tog, yo, k2tog, k1.

Row 12 Yo, k2tog, k18.

Rep rows 1 to 12 until desired length.
Bind off.

don juan's cuff

▶ Cast on 25 sts.

Rows 1 and 2 Knit.

Row 3 Sl 1, k3, [yo, k2tog] 9 times, yo twice, k2tog, k1.

Row 4 K3, p1, k22.

Row 5 Sl 1, k4, [yo, k2tog] 9 times, yo twice, k2tog, k1.

Row 6 K3, p1, k23.

Row 7 Sl 1, k5, [yo, k2tog] 9 times, yo twice, k2tog, k1.

Row 8 K3, p1, k24.

Rows 9 and 11 Sl 1, k27.

Row 10 Knit.

Row 12 Bind off 3 sts, k24.

Rep rows 1 to 12 until desired length.

Bind off.

jester's lace

▶ Cast on 22 sts.
K 1 row.

Row 1 K3, yo twice, k2tog, k10, [yo twice, k2tog] 3 times, k1.

Row 2 K3, p1, [k2, p1] twice, k12, p1, k3.

Rows 3 and 4 Knit.

Row 5 K3, [yo twice, k2tog] twice, k12, [yo twice, k2tog] 3 times, k1.

Row 6 K3, p1, [k2, p1] twice, k14, p1, k2, p1, k3.

Row 7 Knit.

Row 8 K3, k2tog, [k1, k2tog] 8 times, k2.

Row 9 K3, [yo twice, k2tog] 9 times, k1.

Row 10 K3, p1, [k2, p1] 8 times, k3.

Row 11 Knit.

Row 12 K3, [k2tog, k1] 8 times, k2tog, k2.

Row 13 K3, [yo twice, k2tog] 9 times, k1.

Row 14 K3, p1, [k2, p1] 8 times, k3.

Row 15 Knit.

Row 16 Bind off 9 sts, k21.

Rep rows 1 to 16 until desired length.
Bind off.

sock top

▶ Cast on 26 sts.

K 1 row.

Row 1 Sl 1, k19, [yo, k2tog] twice, yo, k2.

Row 2 K8, p14, k5.

Row 3 Sl 1, k6, [yo, k2tog, k1] 4 times, k2, [yo, k2tog] twice, yo, k2.

Row 4 K9, p14, k5.

Row 5 Sl 1, k21, [yo, k2tog] twice, yo, k2.

Row 6 K29.

Row 7 Sl 1, k4, p14, k4, [yo, k2tog] twice, yo, k2.

Row 8 K30.

Row 9 Sl 1, k4, p14, k5, [yo, k2tog] twice, yo, k2.

Row 10 K31.

Row 11 Sl 1, k4, p14, k6, [yo, k2tog] twice, yo, k2.

Row 12 Bind off 6 sts, k25.

Rep rows 1 to 12 until desired length.

Bind off.

lace wheels

▶ Cast on 21 sts.

Row 1 K11, [yo, k2tog] twice, yo 4 times, k2tog twice, yo, k2tog.

Row 2 K4, [k1, p1] twice, k15.

Row 3 K5, k2tog, yo twice, k2tog, k3, [yo, k2tog] twice, k4, k2tog, yo, k1.

Row 4 K16, p1, k6.

Row 5 K3, k2tog, yo twice, k2tog twice, yo twice, k2tog, k2, [yo, k2tog] twice, k3, k2tog, yo, k1.

Row 6 K14, p1, k3, p1, k4.

Row 7 K5, k2tog, yo twice, k2tog, k5, [yo, k2tog] twice, k2, k2tog, yo, k1.

Row 8 Rep row 4.

Row 9 K3, k2tog, yo twice, k2tog twice, yo twice, k2tog, k4, [yo, k2tog] twice, k1, k2tog, yo, k1.

Row 10 Rep row 6.

Row 11 K5, k2tog, yo twice, k2tog, k7, [yo, k2tog] twice, k2tog, yo, k1.

Row 12 Rep row 4.

Row 13 K17, yo, k2tog, yo, k2tog and sl back to LH needle, pass the last 2 sts over this st and sl to the RH needle.

Row 14 Knit.

Rep rows 1 to 14 until desired length.

Bind off.

mary's lace

▶ Cast on 21 sts.

K 1 row.

Row 1 K3, [yo, k2tog] twice, k2, k8 wrapping yarn around each st 4 times, k2, yo 4 times, k2.

Row 2 K3, p1, k1, p1, k2, sl 8 dropping extra wraps, sl the first 4 sts over the last 4 sts and onto the LH needle, then sl the last 4 sts to LH needle and k8, k3, [yo, k2tog] twice, k2.

Rows 3 and 5 K3, [yo, k2tog] twice, k18.

Row 4 K19, [yo, k2tog] twice, k2.

Row 6 Bind off 4 sts, k14, [yo, k2tog] twice, k2.

Rep rows 1 to 6 until desired length.

Bind off.

elizabeth's lace lattice

▶ Cast on 23 sts.

K 1 row.

Row 1 (RS) Sl 1, k2, *yo, k2tog; rep from * to end.

Row 2 K17, p1, k1, p1, k3.

Row 3 Sl 1, k2, [yo, k2tog] twice, k16.

Row 4 K17, p1, k1, p1, k3.

Rows 5 and 9 Sl 1, k2, [yo, k2tog] twice, k16.

Row 6 K1, *yo 4 times, k1; rep from *, to last 6 sts, p1, k1, p1, k3.

Row 7 Sl 1, k2, [yo, k2tog] twice, *drop the 4 yo's, sl next st; rep from * to end—
16 long sts then sl the 16 long sts back to LH needle, [sl sts 5 to 8 over sts 1 to 4 and back to LH needle, k8] twice.

Row 8 K17, p1, k1, p1, k3.

Row 10 Rep row 2.

Rep rows 1 to 10 until desired length, end with row 2.

Bind off.

puff shells

▶ Cast on 20 sts.

Row 1 K3, yo, p2tog, k3, yo, k10, yo, p2tog.

Row 2 Yo, p2tog, k14, yo, p2tog, k3.

Row 3 K3, yo, p2tog, k3, yo, k1, yo, k10, yo, p2tog.

Row 4 Yo, p2tog, k16, yo, p2tog, k3.

Row 5 K3, yo, p2tog, k3, [yo, k1] 3 times, yo, k10, yo, p2tog.

Row 6 Yo, p2tog, k20, yo, p2tog, k3.

Row 7 K3, yo, p2tog, k6, yo, k1, yo, k13, yo, p2tog.

Row 8 Yo, p2tog, k14, yo, k1, yo, k7, yo, p2tog, k3.

Row 9 K3, yo, p2tog, k13, then using point of RH needle [lift 2nd st on left hand needle over first and off needle] 11 times and leave on LH needle, yo, p2tog.

Row 10 Yo, p2tog, k13, yo, p2tog, k3.

Rep row 1 to 10 until desired length.

Bind off.

princess anne's lace

▶ Cast on 13 sts.

Row 1 Sl 1, k5, yo, k2tog tbl, k2tog, yo, k2tog, k1.

Rows 2, 4, 8, 12 and 14 Knit.

Row 3 Sl 1, k3, k2tog, yo, k4, yo, k2.

Row 5 Sl 1, k2, k2tog, yo, k2tog, k1, yo twice, k2tog tbl, k1, yo, k2.

Row 6 K6, p1, k7.

Row 7 Sl 1, k1, k2tog, yo, k8, yo, k2.

Row 9 Sl 1, k2tog, yo, k1, k2tog, yo twice, k2tog tbl, k2tog, yo twice, k2tog tbl, k1, yo, k2.

Row 10 K6, p1, k3, p1, k5.

Row 11 Sl 1, k2, yo, k2tog tbl, k6, k2tog, yo, k2tog, k1.

Row 13 Sl 1, k3, yo, k2tog tbl, k2tog, yo twice, k2tog tbl, k2tog, yo, k2tog, k1.

Row 15 Sl 1, k4, yo, k2tog tbl, k2, k2tog tbl, yo, k2tog, k1.

Row 16 Knit.

Rep rows 1 to 16 until desired length.

Bind off.

beauty and the bead

▶ Cast on 9 sts.

• String 6 beads for each 12 row pat rep.

• Sb 1—Sl 1 bead next to LH needle.

Row 1 (RS) Sb 1, yo, k2tog, yo, k1, yo, ssk, k4.

Row 2 P5, k5.

Row 3 Sb 1, yo, k2tog, yo, k3, yo, ssk, k3.

Row 4 P4, k7.

Row 5 Sb 1, yo, k2tog, yo, k2, ssk, k1, yo, ssk, k2.

Row 6 P3, k1, ssk, yo 3 times, k2tog, k3.

Row 7 Sb l, yo, k2tog, yo, ssk, p1, k1, p1, k2tog, yo, k3.

Row 8 P4, k5, k2tog, k1.

Row 9 Sb 1, yo, k2tog, yo, ssk, k1, k2tog, yo, k4.

Row 10 P5, k3, k2tog, k1.

Row 11 Sb 1, yo, k2tog, yo, s2kp, yo, k5.

Row 12 P6, k1, k2tog, k1.

Rep rows 1 to 12 until desired length.

Bind off.

drop triangles

▲ (multiple of 20 sts plus 5)

Rows 1, 4, 6, 8, 10, 12, 14, 16, 18 K1, p to last 2 sts, k2.

Row 2 (WS) Knit.

Row 3 K2, *k1, yo, k8, p3tog, k8, yo; rep from *, end k3.

Row 5 K2, *k2, yo, k7, p3tog, k7, yo, k1; rep from *, end k3.

Row 7 K2, k2tog, *yo, k1, yo, k6, p3tog, k6, yo, k1, yo, SK2P; rep from *, end last rep k2tog tbl, k2.

Row 9 K2, *k4, yo, k5, p3tog, k5, yo, k3;* rep from *, end k3.

Row 11 K2, *k1, yo, SK2P, yo, k1, yo, k4, p3tog, k4, yo, k1, yo, SK2P, yo; rep from *, end k3.

Row 13 K2, *k6, yo, k3, p3tog, k3, yo, k5; rep from *, end k3.

Row 15 K2, k2tog, *yo, k1, yo, SK2P, yo, k1, yo, k2, p3tog, k2, yo, k1, yo, SK2P, yo, k1, yo, SK2P; rep from *, end last rep k2tog tbl, k2.

Row 17 K2, *k8, yo, k1, p3tog, k1, yo, k7; rep from *, k3.

Row 19 K2, *k1, [yo, SK2P, yo, k1] twice, yo, p3tog, yo, [k1, yo, SK2P, yo] twice; rep from *, end k3.

Row 20 Knit.

Cont as desired.
Make Bobbles I (see page 164) and sew to points.

pyramid

▲ (multiple of 22 sts plus 1)

Bobble Cast on 1 st.

Row 1 [K1, p1] twice, k1—5 sts.

Rows 2 to 8 Sl 1, k4.

Row 9 K2tog, k1, k2tog.

Row 10 K3tog.

Row 11 Place point of left needle into cast on st and k tog with last st. Sl to holder. Make one for each pat rep.

*Cast on 11 sts, sl on bobble, cast on 10 sts; rep from *, end last rep cast on 11 sts.

Row 1 *K1, yo, k9, s2kp, k9, yo; rep from *, end k1.

Row 2 *P2, k19, p1; rep from *, end p1.

Row 3 *K2, yo, k8, s2kp, k8, yo, k1; rep from *, end k1.

Row 4 *P3, k17, p2; rep from *, end p1.

Row 5 *K3, yo, k7, s2kp, k7, yo, k2; rep from *, end k1.

Row 6 *P4, k15, p3; rep from *, end p1.

Row 7 *K4, yo, k6, s2kp, k6, yo, k3; rep from *, end k1.

Row 8 *P5, k13, p4; rep from *, end p1.

Row 9 *K5, yo, k5, s2kp, k5, yo, k4; rep from *, end k1.

Row 10 *P6, k11, p5; rep from *, end p1.

Row 11 *K6, yo, k4, s2kp, k4, yo, k5; rep from *, end k1.

Row 12 *P7, k9, p6; rep from *, end p1.

Row 13 *K7, yo, k3, s2kp, k3, yo, k6; rep from *, end k1.

Row 14 *P8, k7, p7; rep from *, end p1.

Row 15 *K8, yo, k2, s2kp, k2, yo, k7; rep from *, end k1.

Row 16 *P9, k5, p8; rep from *, end p1.

Row 17 *K9, yo, k1, s2kp, k1, yo, k8; rep from *, end k1.

Row 18 *P10, k3, p9; rep from *, end p1.

Row 19 *K10, yo, s2kp, yo, k9; rep from *, end k1.

Row 20 Purl.

Cont as desired.

gazebo lace

▲ (multiple of 10 sts plus 1)

Bobble (MB)

[P1, k1, p1] in next st, [turn, k1, p1, k1] twice, pass 2nd and 3rd st over first st.

Prep row (WS) *P5, MB, p4; rep from *, end last rep p5.

Row 1 K1, *yo, k3, SK2P, k3, yo, k1; rep from * to end.

Row 2 Purl.

Row 3 P1, *k1, yo, k2, SK2P, k2, yo, k1, p1; rep from * to end.

Rows 4 and 6 *K1, p9; rep from *, end k1.

Row 5 P1, *k2, yo, k1, SK2P, k1, yo, k2, p1; rep from * to end.

Row 7 P1, *k3, yo, SK2P, yo, k3, p1; rep from * to end.

Row 8 Purl.

Rows 9 to 16 Rep rows 1 to 8.

Row 17 K1, *k3, yo, SK2P, yo, k4; rep from * to end.

Row 18 Purl.

Rep rows 17 and 18 until desired length.

Cont as desired.

arbor lace

▲ (multiple of 11 sts)

Row 1 (RS) *Ssk, k3 tbl, yo, k1, yo, k3 tbl, k2tog; rep from * to end.

Rows 2, 4, 6 and 8 Purl.

Row 3 *Ssk, k2 tbl, yo, k1, yo, ssk, yo, k2 tbl, k2tog; rep from * to end.

Row 5 *Ssk, k1 tbl, yo, k1, [yo, ssk] twice, yo, k1 tbl, k2tog; rep from * to end.

Row 7 *Ssk, yo, k1, [yo, ssk] 3 times, yo, k2tog; rep from * to end.

Row 9 *K1, p1, k7, p1, k1; rep from * to end.

Row 10 *P1, k1, p7, k1, p1; rep from * to end.

Rep rows 9 and 10 until desired length.

Cont as desired.

fishtail stitch

▲ (multiple of 10 sts plus 3)

Row 1 (RS) K2tog, yo, *k3, SK2P, k3, yo, k1, yo; rep from *, end k1.

Rows 2 and 4 Purl.

Row 3 K2, *yo, k2, SK2P, k2, yo, k3; rep from *, end k1.

Row 5 K2tog, yo, *k1, yo, k1, SK2P, k1, yo, k1, yo, SK2P, yo; rep from *, end k1.

Row 6 Purl.

Rep rows 1 to 6 until desired length.

Cont as desired.

horseshoe with bobbles

▲ (multiple of 10 sts)

Row 1 (RS) *Yo, k3, SP2P, k3, yo, k1; rep from * to end.

Rows 2, 4 and 6 Purl.

Row 3 *K1, yo, k2, SP2P, k2, yo, k2; rep from * to end.

Row 5 *K2, yo, k1, SP2P, k1, yo, k3; rep from * to end.

Row 7 *K3, yo, SP2P, yo, k4 ; rep from * to end.

Row 8 Purl.

Cont as desired.

Make Bobbles (see page 164) and sew to each point.

serendipity

▲ (multiple of 18 sts plus 2)

Row 1 (RS) K1 tbl, *k1 tbl, yo, p2, k2 tbl, p3, p3tog, p3, k2 tbl, p2, yo; rep from *, end k1 tbl.

Row 2 P1 tbl, *yo, p1 tbl, k2, p2 tbl, k2, k3tog, k2, p2 tbl, k2, p1 tbl, yo, p1 tbl; rep from *, end p1 tbl.

Row 3 K1 tbl, *k1 tbl, yo, k2 tbl, p2, k2 tbl, p1, p3tog, p1, k2 tbl, p2, k2 tbl, yo; rep from *, end k1 tbl.

Row 4 P1 tbl, *yo, k1, p2 tbl, k2, p2 tbl, k3tog, p2 tbl, k2, p2 tbl, k1, yo, p1 tbl; rep from *, end p1 tbl.

Row 5 K1 tbl, *k1 tbl, yo, p2, k2 tbl, p2, k1 tbl, k3tog, k1 tbl, p2, k2 tbl, p2, yo; rep from *, end k1 tbl.

Row 6 P1 tbl, *yo, k3, p2 tbl, k2, p3tog, k2, p2 tbl, k3, yo, p1 tbl; rep from *, end p1 tbl.

Row 7 *P3tog, p3, k2 tbl, p2, yo, k1 tbl, yo, p2, k2 tbl, p3; rep from *, end p2tog.

Row 8 K2tog, *k2, p2 tbl, k2, [p1 tbl, yo] twice, p1 tbl, k2, p2 tbl, k2, k3tog; rep from *, end last rep k2tog.

Row 9 P2tog, p1, k2 tbl, p2, k2 tbl, yo, k1 tbl, yo, k2 tbl, p2, k2 tbl, p1, *p3tog, p1, k2 tbl, p2, k2 tbl, yo, k1 tbl, yo, k2 tbl, p2, k2 tbl, p1; rep from *, end p2tog.

Row 10 P2tog tbl, *p2 tbl, k2, p2 tbl, k1, yo, p1 tbl, yo, k1, p2 tbl, k2, p2 tbl, k3tog; rep from *, end last rep k2tog.

Row 11 K2tog, k1 tbl, p2, k2 tbl, p2, yo, k1 tbl, yo, p2, k2 tbl, p2, k1 tbl, *k3tog, k1 tbl, p2, k2 tbl, p2, yo, k1 tbl, yo, p2, k2 tbl, p2, k1 tbl; rep from *, end k2tog tbl.

Row 12 K2tog, *k2, p2 tbl, k3, yo, p1 tbl, yo, k3, p2 tbl, k2, p3tog; rep from *, end last rep p2.

Cont as desired.

lozenge lattice

▲ (multiple of 12 sts plus 4)

Bobble

Cast on 1 st.

Row 1 [K1, p1] twice, k1 in same st—5 sts.

Rows 2 and 4 K5.

Rows 3 and 5 P5.

Row 6 K5, pass 2nd, 3rd, 4th and 5th st over first st. Insert point of LH needle into cast on st, sl last st on RH needle to LH needle and k2tog. Put rem st on holder. Make 1 bobble for each pat rep.

Cast on 8 sts, *sl bobble from holder, cast on 11 sts; rep from *, end sl bobble from holder, cast on 7 sts.

Row 1 and all WS rows Purl.

Row 2 K3, *k4, [yo, ssk] twice, k4; rep from *, end last rep k5.

Row 4 K3, *k2, ssk, yo, k1, [yo, k2tog] twice, k3; rep from *, end last rep k4.

Row 6 K3, *k1, [ssk, yo] twice, k1, [yo, k2tog] twice, k2; rep from *, end last rep k3.

Row 8 K3, *[ssk, yo] twice, k3, [yo, k2tog] twice, k1; rep from *, end last rep k2.

Row 10 K2, ssk *yo, ssk, yo, k5, yo, k2tog, yo, k3tog; rep from *, end last rep yo, ssk, yo, k5, [yo, k2tog] twice, k1.

Row 12 K1, ssk, yo, *ssk, yo, k7, yo, k3tog, yo; rep from *, end k1.

Row 14 Ssk, yo, ssk, *yo, k8, ssk, yo, ssk; rep from *, end yo, k8, ssk, yo, k2.

Row 16 K1, ssk, yo, *k1, yo, k2tog, k5, [ssk, yo] twice; rep from *, end k1.

Row 18 Ssk, yo, k1, *[yo, k2tog] twice, k3, [ssk, yo] twice, k1; rep from *, end last rep k2.

Row 20 K3, *k1, [yo, k2tog] twice, k1, [ssk, yo] twice, k2; rep from *, end last rep k3.

Row 22 K3, *k2, yo, ssk, yo, SK2P, yo, k2tog, yo, k3; rep from *, end last rep k4.

Row 24 K3, *k3, yo, ssk, yo, SK2P, yo, k4; rep from *, end last rep k5.

Cont as desired.

casey's picot point

▲ (multiple of 20 sts plus 1)

Cast on using the provisional method. (See pg 166.)

Rows 1, 3, 5 and 7 (RS) Knit.

Rows 2 and 6 Purl.

Row 4 P1, *yo, p2tog; rep from * to end.

Row 8 Fold hem at picot edge. Place cast on sts on a spare needle and hold parallel to working needle, insert a third needle into the first st on each needle and p them tog, cont across row.

Row 9 *K1, yo, [p1, k1 tbl] 4 times, SK2P, [k1 tbl, p1] 4 times, yo; rep from *, end k1.

Row 10 P1, *p1, yo, [k1, p1 tbl] 3 times, k1, SP2P, k1, [p1 tbl, k1] 3 times, yo, p2; rep from * to end.

Row 11 *K3, yo, [p1, k1 tbl] 3 times, SK2P, [k1 tbl, p1] 3 times, yo, k2; rep from *, end last rep k3.

Row 12 P1, *p3, yo, [k1, p1 tbl] twice, k1, SP2P, k1, [p1 tbl, k1] twice, yo, p4; rep from * to end.

Row 13 *K5, yo, [p1, k1 tbl] twice, SK2P, [k1 tbl, p1] twice, yo, k4; rep from *, end last rep k5.

Row 14 P1, *p5, yo, k1, p1 tbl, k1, SP2P, k1, p1 tbl, k1, yo, p6; rep from * to end.

Row 15 *K7, yo, p1, k1 tbl, SK2P, k1 tbl, p1, yo, k6; rep from *, end last rep k7.

Row 16 P1, *p7, yo, k1, SP2P, k1, yo, p8; rep from * to end.

Row 17 *K9, yo, SK2P, yo, k8; rep from *, end last rep k9.

Row 18 Purl.

Cont as desired.

victoria's lace picot

▲ (multiple of 15 sts plus 6)

• Cast on using the provisional cast-on method (see page 166).

Rows 1, 3, 5 and 7 (RS) Knit.

Rows 2 and 6 Purl.

Row 4 P1, *yo, p2tog; rep from * to end.

Row 8 Fold hem at picot edge. Place cast-on sts on a spare needle and hold parallel to working needle, insert a third needle into the first st on each needle and p them tog, cont across row.

Row 9 K1, *k2, yo, ssk, yo, [k1 tbl, p1] twice, SK2P, [p1, k1 tbl] twice, yo; rep from * to last 5 sts, end k2tog, yo, k3.

Row 10 P1, p2tog, yo, p2, *p1 tbl, yo, p1 tbl, k1, p1 tbl, SP2P, p1 tbl, k1, p1 tbl, yo, p1 tbl, p2, yo, ssp; rep from *, end p1.

Row 11 K1, *k2, yo, ssk, k1 tbl, p1, yo, k1 tbl, p1, SK2P, p1, k1 tbl, yo, p1, k1 tbl; rep from * to last 5 sts, end k2tog, yo, k3.

Row 12 P1, p2tog, yo, p2, *p1 tbl, k1, p1 tbl, yo, p1 tbl, SP2P, p1 tbl, yo, p1 tbl, k1, p1 tbl, p2, yo, ssp; rep from *, end p1.

Row 13 K1, *k2, yo, ssk, [k1 tbl, p1] twice, yo, SK2P, yo, [p1, k1 tbl] twice; rep from * to last 5 sts, end k2tog, yo, k3.

Row 14 P1, p2tog, yo, p2, *yo, [p1 tbl, k1] twice, SP2P, [k1, p1 tbl] twice, yo, p2, yo, ssp; rep from *, end p1.

Row 15 K1, *k2, yo, ssk, k1 tbl, yo, k1 tbl, p1, k1 tbl, SK2P, k1 tbl, p1, k1 tbl, yo, k1 tbl; rep from * to last 5 sts, end k2tog, yo, k3.

Row 16 P1, p2tog, yo, p2, *p1 tbl, k1, yo, p1 tbl, k1, SP2P, k1, p1 tbl, yo, k1, p1 tbl, p2, yo, ssp; rep from *, end p1.

Row 17 K1, *k2, yo, ssk, k1 tbl, p1, k1 tbl, yo, k1 tbl, SK2P, k1 tbl, yo, k1 tbl, p1, k1 tbl; rep from * to last 5 sts, end k2tog, yo, k3.

Row 18 P1, p2tog, yo, p2, *[p1 tbl, k1] twice, yo, SP2P, yo, [k1, p1 tbl] twice, p2, yo, ssp; rep from *, end p1.

Cont as desired.

eyelet bead picot

▲ (multiple of 8 sts plus 1)

• Cast on using provisional method (see page 166).

Rows 1, 3, 5 and 7 (RS) Knit.

Rows 2 and 6 Purl.

Row 4 P1, *yo, p2tog; rep from * to end.

Row 8 Fold hem at picot edge. Place cast-on sts on a spare needle and hold parallel to working needle, insert a third needle into the first st on each needle and p them tog, cont across row.

Row 9 K2, *yo, k2tog; rep from *, end k1.

Rows 10 and 12 Purl.

Row 11 Knit.

Row 13 K1, yo, *ssk, k3, k2tog, yo, k1, yo; rep from *, end ssk, k3, k2tog, yo, k1.

Row 14 P2, yo, p2tog, k1, p2tog tbl, yo, *p3, yo, p2tog, p1, p2tog tbl, yo; rep from *, end p2.

Row 15 K2, *k1, yo, k3tog, yo, k4; rep from *, end last rep k3.

Row 16 P2, p2tog tbl, yo, p1, yo, p2tog, *p3, p2tog tbl, yo, p1, yo, p2tog; rep from *, end p2.

Row 17 K1, k2tog, *yo, k3, yo, ssk, k1, k2tog; rep from *, end last rep yo, k3, yo, ssk, k1.

Row 18 P2tog tbl, yo, k5, *yo, p3tog, yo, p5; rep from *, end yo, p2tog.

Row 19 Knit.

Row 20 Purl.

Row 21 Rep row 9.

Work 5 rows in St st.

Cont as desired.

feather lace

▲ (multiple of 9 sts plus 4)

Rows 1 and 3 (WS) Purl.

Row 2 K3, *yo, k2, ssk, k2tog, k2, yo, k1; rep from *, end last rep k2.

Row 4 K2, *yo, k2, ssk, k2tog, k2, yo, k1; rep from *, end last rep k3.

Rep rows 1 to 4 until desired length.

Cont as desired.

scalloped feather lace

▲ (multiple of 9 sts plus 4)

Rows 1, 2 and 3 Knit.

Rows 4 and 6 Purl.

Row 5 K3, *yo, k2, ssk, k2tog, k2, yo, k1; rep from *, end last rep k2.

Row 7 K2, *yo, k2, ssk, k2tog, k2, yo, k1; rep from *, end last rep k3.

Row 8 Purl.

Rep rows 5 to 8 until desired length.

Cont as desired.

quill eyelet

 (multiple of 6 sts plus 1)

Row 1 (WS) Purl.

Row 2 K1, *yo, k1, SK2P, k1, yo, k1; rep from * to end.

Rep rows 1 and 2 until desired length.

Cont as desired.

old fan shell

▲ (multiple of 15 sts plus 4)

Row 1 (WS) P4, *k11, p4; rep from * to end.

Row 2 K4, *p11, k4; rep from * to end.

Row 3 P2, *p2tog, p11, p2tog tbl; rep from *, end p2.

Row 4 K2, *ssk, k9, k2tog; rep from *, end k2.

Row 5 P2, *p2tog, p7, p2tog tbl; rep from *, end p2.

Row 6 K4, *[yo, k1] 5 times, yo, k4; rep from * to end.

Rep rows 1 to 6 until desired length.

Cont as desired.

razor eyelet

▲ (multiple of 12 sts plus 1)

Row 1 (WS) Purl.

Row 2 K1, *yo, k4, SK2P, k4, yo, k1; rep from * to end.

Rep rows 1 and 2 until desired length.

Cont as desired.

fan fair

🔺 (multiple of 18 sts)

K 2 rows.

Row 1 (RS) Knit.

Row 2 Purl.

Row 3 *K2tog 3 times, [yo, k1] 6 times, k2tog 3 times; rep from * to end.

Row 4 Knit.

Rep rows 1 to 4 until desired length.

Cont as desired.

madeira scallop

🔺 (multiple of 18 sts plus 1)

Row 1 *K1, k2tog 3 times, [yo, k1] 5 times, yo, k2tog tbl 3 times; rep from *, end k1.

Rows 2 and 4 Purl.

Row 3 Knit.

Rep rows 1 to 4 until desired length.

Cont as desired.

petite shells

 (beg as a multiple of 5 sts plus 2 and end as a multiple of 4 sts plus 1)

Row 1 (RS) K1, yo, *k5, sl the 2nd, 3rd, 4th, and 5th st over the first st, yo; rep from *, k1.

Row 2 P1, *[p1, yo, k1 tbl] in next st, p1; rep from * to end.

Row 3 K2, k1 tbl, *k3, k1 tbl; rep from *, end k2.

K 3 rows.

Cont as desired.

lacy shells

◢ (beg as a multiple of 5 sts plus 2 and end as a multiple of 4 sts plus 1)

Row 1 (RS) K1, yo, *k5, sl the 2nd, 3rd and 4th and 5th st over the first st, yo; rep from *, end k1.

Row 2 P1, *[p1, yo, k1 tbl] in next st, p1; rep from * to end.

Row 3 K2, k1 tbl, *k3, k1 tbl; rep from *, end k2.

Row 4 Knit.

Rows 5, 6 and 7 K1, *yo, k2tog; rep from * to end.

Row 8 Knit.

Cont as desired.

fan dance

▲ (multiple of 19 sts)

Rows 1 and 2 Knit.

Row 3 *K1, yo twice, ssp, k13, p2tog, yo twice, k1; rep from * to end.

Row 4 *K2, p1, k15, p1, k2; rep from * to end.

Rows 5 and 6 Knit.

Row 7 *K1, [yo twice, ssp] twice, k11, [p2tog, yo twice] twice, k1; rep from * to end.

Row 8 *[K2, p1] twice, k13, [p1, k2] twice; rep from * to end.

Row 9 Knit.

Row 10 *K6, [yo twice, k1] 14 times, k5; rep from * to end.

Row 11 *K1, [yo twice, ssp] twice, yo twice, dropping extra yo's of previous row, p15tog, yo twice, [p2tog, yo twice] twice, k1; rep from * to end.

Row 12 *K1, [p1, k1] 4 times, k1, [k1, p1] 4 times, k1; rep from * to end.

Cont as desired.

lacy shells (with ribbons)

Thread ribbon through holes.

dotted chevrons

▲ (multiple of 20 sts plus 1)

• **Make Bobble** (MB)

[K1, p1] twice, k1 in next st, turn, k5, turn, bind off 4 sts.

Row 1 (RS) K1, *yo, SKP, k15, k2tog, yo, k1; rep from * to end.

Row 2 K1, p1, *yo, p2tog, p13, p2tog, yo, p3; rep from *, end last rep p1, k1.

Row 3 K3, *yo, SKP, k11, k2tog, yo, k5; rep from *, end last rep k3.

Row 4 K1, p3, *yo, p2tog, p9, p2tog, yo, p7; rep from *, end last rep p3, k1.

Row 5 K5, *yo SKP, k3, MB, k3, k2tog, yo, k9; rep from *, end last rep k5.

Row 6 K1, p5, *yo, p2tog, p5, p2tog, yo, p11; rep from *, end last rep p5, k1.

Row 7 K7, *yo, SKP, k3, k2tog, yo, k6, MB, k6; rep from *, end last rep k7.

Row 8 K1, p7, *yo, p2tog, p1, p2tog, yo, p15; rep from *, end last rep p7, k1.

Rep rows 1 to 8 until desired length.

Cont as desired.

lace triangles

▲ (multiple of 11 sts plus 5)

Row 1 (RS) *K3, [yo, SKP] 4 times; rep from *, end k5.

Row 2 and all WS rows Purl.

Row 3 *K4, [yo, SKP] 3 times, k1; rep from *, end k5.

Row 5 *K5, [yo, SKP] twice, k2; rep from *, end k5.

Row 7 *K6, yo, SKP, k3; rep from *, end k5.

Row 9 K5, *k3, [yo, SKP] 4 times; rep from * to end.

Row 11 K5, *k4, [yo, SKP] 3 times, k1; rep from * to end.

Row 13 K5, *k5, [yo, SKP] twice, k2; rep from * to end.

Row 15 K5, *k6, yo, SKP, k3; rep from * to end.

Cont as desired.

persian lace poles

▲ (multiple of 8 sts plus 2)

Rows 1, 3, 5 and 7 (RS) K1, p3, *k2, p6; rep from *, end last rep p3, k1.

Rows 2, 4, 6 and 8 K4, p2, *k6, p2; rep from *, end k4.

Row 9 K1, p2, *k2tog, yo, ssk, p4; rep from *, end last rep p3.

Row 10 K3, *p1, inc 1, p1, k4; rep from *, end last rep k3.

Row 11 K1, p1, *k2tog, yo, k2, yo, ssk, p2; rep from * to end.

Row 12 K2, *p6, k2; rep from * to end.

Row 13 K1, *[k2tog, yo] twice, ssk, yo, ssk; rep from *, end k1.

Row 14 K1, p3, *inc 1, p6; rep from *, end last rep p4.

Row 15 K1, *[yo, ssk] twice, k2tog, yo, k2tog; rep from *, end yo, k1.

Row 16 K1, k1 tbl, p6, *inc 1, p6; rep from *, end, k1 tbl, k1.

Row 17 K1, p1, *yo, SK2P, yo, k3tog, yo, p2; rep from * to end.

Row 18 K2, *k1 tbl, p1, inc 1, p1, k1 tbl, k2; rep from * to end.

Row 19 K1, p2, *yo, ssk, k2tog, yo, p4; rep from *, end last rep p2, k1.

Row 20 K3, *k1 tbl, p2, k1 tbl, k4; rep from *, end last rep k3.

Rep rows 1 to 4 until desired length.

Cont as desired.

italian lace ladder cable

▲ (multiple of 7 sts plus 6)

Row 1 (RS) K1, *k2tog, yo twice, ssk, k3; rep from *, end last rep k1.

Row 2 K1, *k1, k1 tbl, k2, p3; rep from *, end last rep p1.

Row 3 K1, *k2tog, yo twice, ssk, skip next 2 sts and k 3rd st, then k 2nd st, then k first st, then sl all 3 sts from needle tog; rep from *, end k2tog, yo twice, ssk, k1.

Row 4 Rep row 2.

Rep rows 1 to 4 twice more.

Cont as desired.

lace cable twist

▲ (multiple of 11 sts plus 7)

Row 1 and all WS rows Purl.

Row 2 K1, *yo, ssk, k1, k2tog, yo, k6; rep from *, end last rep k1.

Row 4 K2, *yo, SK2P, yo, k1, 6-st RC, k1; rep from *, end yo, SK2P, yo, k2.

Row 6 Rep row 2.

Row 8 K2, *yo, SK2P, yo, k8; rep from *, end last rep k2.

Rep rows 1 to 8 until desired length.

Cont as desired.

cable chevron

▲ (multiple of 19 sts plus 2)

K 3 rows.

Row 1 (RS) *P2, k4 tbl, k1, yo, k2tog tbl, k3, k2tog, yo, k1, k4 tbl; rep from *, end p2.

Rows 2, 4, and 6 *K2, p4 tbl, k1, p7, k1, p4 tbl; rep from *, end k2.

Row 3 *P2, k4 tbl, k2, yo, k2tog tbl, k1, k2tog, yo, k2, k4 tbl; rep from *, end p2.

Row 5 *P2, 4-st LTC, k3, yo, sk2p, yo, k3, 4-st RTC; rep from *, end p2.

Row 7 *P2, k4 tbl, k9, k4 tbl; rep from *, end p2.

Row 8 Rep row 2.

Rep rows 1 to 8 twice more.

K 3 rows.

Cont as desired.

four sisters

▲ (multiple of 15 sts)

Row 1 (RS) *K5, k2tog, yo, k1, yo, ssk, k5; rep from * to end.

Row 2 *P4, p2tog tbl, yo, p3, yo, p2tog, p4; rep from * to end.

Row 3 *K3, k2tog, yo, k5, yo, ssk, k3; rep from * to end.

Row 4 *P2, p2tog tbl, yo, p1, yo, p2tog, p1, p2tog tbl, yo, p1, yo, p2tog, p2; rep from * to end.

Row 5 *K1, k2tog, yo, k3, yo, k3tog, yo, k3, yo, ssk, k1; rep from * to end.

Row 6 *P2, yo, p5, yo, p1, yo, p5, yo, p2; rep from * to end.

Row 7 *[K3, yo, ssk, k1, k2tog, yo] twice, k3; rep from * to end.

Row 8 *P4, p3tog, yo, p5, yo, p3tog, p4; rep from * to end.

Row 9 *K6, yo, ssk, k1, k2tog, yo, k6; rep from * to end.

Row 10 *P3, p2tog tbl, p2, yo, p3tog, yo, p2, p2tog, p3; rep from * to end.

Rep rows 1 to 10 until desired length.

Cont as desired.

Add tassels at lower edge (see photo).

bead stitch

▲ (multiple of 7 sts)

Row 1 (RS) *K1, k2tog, yo, k1, yo, ssk, k1; rep from * to end.

Row 2 *P2tog tbl, yo, p3, yo, p2tog; rep from * to end.

Row 3 *K1, yo, ssk, k1, k2tog, yo, k1; rep from * to end.

Row 4 *P2, yo, p3tog, yo, p2; rep from * to end.

Rep rows 1 to 4 until desired length. Cont as desired.

cogwheel

▲ (beg as a multiple of 8 sts plus 5)

Increase in Row Below (inc 1-b)
K into back of st 1 row below next st then k next st on needle.
K 2 rows.

Row 1 and all WS rows Purl.

Row 2 K3, *sl 3 sts to cn, wrap yarn clockwise around these 3 sts once, sl to RH needle and k them, k1; rep from *, end k2.

Row 4 K1, k3tog, yo, [k1, yo, k1 tbl] in next st, *yo, k3tog tbl, k1, k3tog, yo, [k1, yo, k1 tbl] in next st; rep from *, end yo, k3tog, k5.

Row 6 [K2tog, yo] twice, k1 tbl, *yo, ssk, yo, SK2P, yo, k2tog, yo, k1 tbl; rep from * to last 8 sts, end [yo, ssk] twice, k4.

Row 8 K1, yo, k2tog, yo, SK2P, *yo, ssk, yo, k1, yo, k2tog, yo, SK2P; rep from * to last 7 sts, end yo, ssk, yo, k5.

Row 10 [Ssk, yo] twice, k1 tbl, *yo, k2tog, yo, SK2P, yo, ssk, yo, k1 tbl; rep from * to last 8 sts, end [yo, k2tog] twice, k4.

Row 12 K1, inc 1-b, yo, dec 4, *yo, inc 1-b, k1, inc 1-b, yo, dec 4; rep from *, end yo, inc 1-b, k5.

Row 14 Rep row 2.

Row 15 Purl.
K 2 rows.
Cont as desired.

fringes

loop-d-loop

▲ (multiple of 2 sts plus 1)

• Loops are formed as the background is worked.

Rows 1 to 6 Knit.

Row 7 *K1, k next st wrapping yarn 4 times; rep from *, end k1.

Row 8 *K1, k next st dropping 3 extra loops from each yo; rep from *, end k1.

Rep rows 1 to 8 for each row of fringe. Bind off all sts.

Apply a Traditional Single Knot Fringe to each loop section.

traditional fringe braided

Work as for Traditional Single Knot Fringe, braiding ends. Tie ends of each braid to secure.

traditional single knot fringe

Note See art work on page 166.

Cut several strands of yarn (the more strands, the thicker the fringe) twice the desired fringe length, plus 1"/2.5cm for knotting. Insert a crochet hook from back to front through knitted piece and folded yarn. Pull yarn through the knitting. Draw ends and tighten. Trim ends even.

Unraveled Fringes

These are fringes that are worked into the knitted edge, then unraveled after the edge is completed, instead of a traditional applied fringe. The length of the fringe is determined by the number of extra stitches not included in the pattern repeat as well as the weight of the yarn. To lengthen or shorten fringe, cast on more or fewer stitches. You can work these extra stitches in either stockinette stitch or garter stitch. After the fringe is unraveled it can be cut, twisted, braided or left looped.

garter stitch fringe

▶ Cast on 16 sts.

Work in garter st until desired length.

Bind off 7 sts, fasten off 8th st.

Sl rem 8 sts off needle and unravel them on every row.

Working from right to left, knot loops of 6 adjacent rows.

seed stich fringe

▶ Cast on 17 sts.

Row 1 *K1, p1; rep from *, end k1.

Rep row 1 until desired length.

Bind off 8 sts, fasten off 9th st.

Sl rem 8 sts off needle and unravel them on every row for fringe.

Cut loops and trim.

two-color fringe

▶ With 1 strand each of A and B held tog, cast on 12 sts.

Row 1 (RS) K2, yo, k2tog, k1, yo, k2tog, k5.

Row 2 P4, k2, [yo, k2tog, k1] twice.

Rep rows 1 and 2 until desired length, end with a RS row.

Bind off 7 sts, fasten off 8th st.

Sl rem 4 sts off needle and unravel them on every row for fringe.

Cut loops and trim.

cockleshells

▲ (multiple of 10 sts plus 3)

Note: To K1B over the yo's on rows 4, 8, 12 and 16, insert the needle into yo space 1 row below, and knit.

Row 1 (WS) Knit.

Row 2 P2, * p4, yo, p1, yo, p5; rep from *, end p1.

Row 3 K1, *k5, p1, k1, p1, k4; rep from *, end k2.

Row 4 P2, *p4, k1B, p1, k1B, p5; rep from *, end p1.

Row 5 Rep row 3.

Row 6 P2, *p3, yo, p1, [k1B, p1] twice, yo, p4; rep from *, end p1.

Row 7 K1, *k4, [p1, k1] 4 times, k2; rep from *, end k2.

Row 8 P2, *p3, [k1B, p1] 4 times, p3; rep from *, end p1.

Row 9 Rep row 7.

Row 10 P2, *p2, yo, [p1, k1B] 4 times, p1, yo, p3; rep from *, end p1.

Row 11 K1, *k3, [p1, k1] 6 times, k1; rep from *, end k2.

Row 12 P2, *p2, [k1B, p1] 6 times, p2; rep from *, end p1.

Row 13 Rep row 11.

Row 14 P2, *p1, yo, [p1, k1B] 6 times, p1, yo, p2; rep from *, end p1.

Row 15 K1, *k2, [p1, k1] 8 times; rep from *, end k2.

Row 16 P2, *[p1, k1B] 8 times, p2; rep from *, end p1.

Row 17 Rep row 15.

Row 18 P2, *p1, p2tog 8 times, p1; rep from *, end p1.

Cont as desired.

Apply a Single Knot Fringe at each point.

wheat spray

▲ MB

[K1, p1, k1, p1, k1] in one st—5 sts, then pass 2nd, 3rd, 4th and 5th sts, one at a time, over first st.

(multiple of 11sts plus 2)

Row 1 (RS) P2, *p4, k1, p6; rep from * to end.

Row 2 *K6, p1, k4; rep from *, end k2.

Row 3 P2, *p2, k1 [p1, k1] twice, p4; rep from * to end.

Row 4 *K4, p1, [k1, p1] twice, k2; rep from *, end k2.

Row 5 P2, *[k1, p1] 4 times, k1, p2; rep from * to end.

Row 6 *K2, [p1, k1] 4 times, p1; rep from *, end k2.

Rows 7, 9 and 11 Rep row 5.

Rows 8, 10 and 12 Rep row 6.

Row 13 P2, *sl next 6 sts to cn and hold to back, k1, p1, k1, then [p1, k1] 3 times from cn, p2; rep from * to end.

Rows 14 and 16 Rep row 6.

Row 15 Rep row 5.

Row 17 P2, *MB, [p1, k1] 3 times, p1, MB, p2; rep from * to end.

Row 18 *K4, [p1, k1] twice, p1, k2; rep from *, end k2.

Row 19 P2, *p2, MB, p1, k1, p1, MB, p4; rep from * to end.

Row 20 *K6, p1, k4; rep from *, end k2.

Row 21 P2, *p4, MB, p6; rep from * to end.

Row 22 Knit.

Cont as desired.

Fringe: Cut 6 pieces of yarn 6"/15cm long, fold in half and attach to knit st on first row.

petruchio tassel border

▲ (multiple of 12 sts plus 1)

• When making tassel (MT) wind yarn around 4 fingers instead of 2.

Cast on with A.

Row 1 (RS) Work in seed st.

Row 2 With A, work 6 sts in seed st, *with B make tassel, with A work 11 sts in seed st; rep from *, end last rep with A, work 6 sts in seed st.

Row 3 With A, work 6 sts in seed st, *k1 B, with A, work 11 sts in seed st; rep from *, end last rep with A, work 6 sts in seed st.

Row 4 With A, work 5 sts in seed st, *p3 B, with A, work 9 sts in seed st; rep from *, end last rep with A, work 5 sts in seed st.

Row 5 With A, work 4 sts in seed st, *k5 B, with A, work 7 sts in seed st; rep from *, end last rep with A, work 4 sts in seed st.

Row 6 With A, work 3 sts in seed st, *p7 B, with A, work 5 sts in seed st; rep from *, end last rep with A, work 3 sts in seed st.

Row 7 With A, work 2 sts in seed st, *k9 B, with A, work 3 sts in seed st; rep from *, end last rep with A, work 2 sts in seed st.

Row 8 With A, work 1 st in seed st, *p11 B, with A, work 1 st in seed st; rep from * to end.

Row 9 *K1 A, k11 B; rep from *, end k1 A.

Cont in St st and colors as established until desired length.

Cut and trim tassels.

romeo's tassel border

▲ (multiple of 11 sts plus 2)

Row 1 (RS) Purl.

Row 2 K6, *MT, k10; rep from *, end last rep k6.

Row 3 P6, *inc 1 in tassel st, p10; rep from *, end last rep p6.

Row 4 K6, *p2, k10; rep from *, end last rep k6.

Row 5 P5, *1/1 RPC, 1/1 LPC, p8; rep from *, end last rep p5.

Row 6 and all WS rows K the knit sts and p the purl sts.

Row 7 P4, *1/1 RPC, p2, 1/1 LPC, p6; rep from *, end last rep p4.

Row 9 P3, *1/1 RPC, p4, 1/1 LPC, p4; rep from *, end last rep p3.

Row 11 P2 *1/1 RPC, p6, 1/1 LPC, p2; rep from *, to end.

Row 13 P1, *l/1 RPC, p8, 1/1 LPC; rep from * end p1.

Row 15 P1, k1 *p10, 2-st LC; rep from *, end p10, k1, p1.

Row 17 P1, *1/1 LPC, p8, 1/1 RPC; rep from *, end p1.

Row 19 P2, *1/1 LPC, p6, 1/1 RPC, p2; rep from *, to end.

Row 21 P3, *1/1 LPC, p4, 1/1 RPC, p4; rep form *, end last rep p3.

Row 23 P4, *1/1 LPC, p2, 1/1 RPC, p6; rep from *, end last rep p4.

Row 25 P5, *1/1 LPC, 1/1 RPC, p8; rep from *, end last rep p5.

Row 27 P6, *k2tog, p10; rep from *, end last rep p6.

Beg with a WS row and work in rev St st or cont as desired. If desired, embroider a daisy st (p 166) in each diamond section.

juliet's tassel border

▲ (beg as a multiple of 11 sts plus 1 and end as a multiple of 12 sts)

Row 1 (RS) Purl.

Row 2 K5 *p2, k4, MT, k4; rep from *, end last rep p2, k5.

Row 3 P5, *2-st RC, p4, inc 1, p4; rep from *, end last rep 2-st RC, p5.

Row 4 and all WS rows K the knit sts and p the purl sts.

Row 5 P4, *2-st RC, 2-st LC, P8; rep from *, end last rep p4.

Row 7 P3, *2-st RC, k2, 2-st LC, p6; rep from *, end last rep p3.

Row 9 P2, *2-st RC, k4, 2-st LC, p4; rep from *, end last rep p2.

Row 11 P1, *2-st RC, k6, 2-st LC, p2; rep from *, end last rep p1.

Row 13 *2-st RC, k8, 2-st LC ; rep from *, to end.

Row 15 K11, *2-st RC, k10; rep from * end last rep k11.

Beg with a WS row and work in St st or cont as desired.

Cut and trim tassels.

twin cable

▶ Cast on 29 sts.

Rows 1 and 3 (RS) K6, k2tog, yo, [p2, k6] twice, p2, yo, k2tog, k1.

Row 2 and all WS rows K5, p6, k2, p6, k10.

Row 5 K6, k2tog, yo, [p2, 6-st LC] twice, p2, yo, k2tog, k1.

Row 7 Rep row 1.

Row 8 Rep row 2.

Rep rows 1 to 8 until desired length, end with a RS row.

Bind off 23 sts, fasten off 24th st.

Sl rem 5 sts off needle and unravel them on every row for fringe.

Cut loops and trim.

split cable

▶ With A, cast on 21 sts.

Row 1 (RS) K12 A, with B, p1, k1, p1, k6 A.

Rows 2 and 4 P6 A, with B, p1, k1, p1, p12 A.

Row 3 With A, k6, 6-st RC, with B, p1, k1, p1, with A 6-st LC.

Rep rows 1 to 4 until desired length.

Bind off 14 sts, fasten off 15th st.

Sl rem 6 sts off needle and unravel them on every row for fringe.

Cut loops and trim.

contrast cable

▶ Cast on 9 sts with A and 5 sts with B—14 sts.

Rows 1 and 5 (RS) K5 B, k9 A.

Row 2 and all WS rows P9 A, p5 B.

Row 3 K5 B, with A 6-st LC, k3.

Row 7 K5 B, with A, k3, 6-st RC.

Row 8 Rep row 2.

Rep rows 1 to 8 until desired length, end with a RS row.

Bind off 9 sts, fasten off 10th st.

Sl rem 4 sts off needle and unravel them on every row for fringe.

Cut loops and trim.

woven braid

▶ Cast on 22 sts.

Rows 1 and 5 Knit.

Row 2 and all WS rows Purl.

Row 3 K7, 6-st LC twice, k3.

Row 7 K4, 6-st RC 3 times.

Row 8 Purl.

Rep rows 1 to 8 until desired length, end with a RS row.

Bind off 17 sts, fasten off 18th st.

Sl rem 4 sts off needle and unravel them on every row for fringe.

celtic princess braid

▶ Cast on 34 sts.

Prep row (WS) P1, k3, [p6, k4] twice, p3, k1, p6.

Row 1 K6, p1, k3, [p4, 6-st LC] twice, p3, k1.

Row 2 and all WS rows K the knit sts and p the purl sts.

Row 3 K6, p1, [3/2 LPC, 3/2 RPC] twice, 3/2 LPC, p1, k1.

Row 5 K6, p3, [6-st RC, p4] twice, k3, p1, k1.

Row 7 K6, p1, [3/2 RPC, 3/2 LPC] twice, 3/2 RPC, p1, k1.

Rep rows 1 to 8 until desired length, end with a RS row.

Bind off 27 sts, fasten off 28th st.

Sl rem 6 sts off needle and unravel them on every row for fringe.

Cut loops and trim.

saxon braid

▶ Cast on 35 sts.

Rows 1 and 3 (WS) P1, k4 [p4, k4] 3 times, p1, p5.

Row 2 K5, k1 tbl [p4, 4-st RC] 3 times, p4, k1 tbl.

Row 4 K5, k1 tbl, p3, 2/1 RPC, [2/2 LPC, 2/2 RPC] twice, 2/1 LPC, p3, k1 tbl.

Row 5 P1, k3, p2, k3, p4, k4, p4, k3, p2, k3, p1, p5.

Row 6 K5, k1 tbl, p3, 2/1 RPC, p2, 4-st LC, p4, 4-st LC, p3, 2/1 LPC, p2, k1 tbl.

Row 7 P1, k2, p2, [k4, p4] twice, k4, p2, k2, p1, p5.

Row 8 K5, k1 tbl, p2, k2, p2, [2/2 RPC, 2/2 LPC] twice, p2, k2, p2, k1 tbl.

Row 9 P1, [k2, p2] twice, k4, p4, k4 [p2, k2] twice, p1, p5.

Row 10 K5, k1 tbl, [p2, k2] twice, p4, 4-st RC, p4, [k2, p2] twice, k1 tbl.

Row 11 Rep row 9.

Row 12 K5, k1 tbl, p2, k2, p2, [2/2 LPC, 2/2 RPC] twice, p2, k2, p2, k1 tbl.

Row 13 P1, k2, p2, [k4, p4] twice, k4, p2, k2, p1, p5.

Row 14 K5, k1 tbl, p3, 2/1 RPC, p2, 4-st LC, p4, 4-st LC, p3, 2/1 LPC, p2, k1 tbl.

Row 15 P1, k3, p2, k3, p4, k4, p4, k3, p2, k3, p1, p5.

Row 16 K5, k1 tbl, p3, 2/1 LPC, [2/2 RPC, 2/2 LPC] twice, 2/1 RPC, p3, k1 tbl.

Rep rows 1 to 16 until desired length, end with a RS row.

Bind off 29 sts, fasten off 30th st.

Sl rem 5 sts off needle and unravel them on every row for fringe.

Cut loops and trim.

balanced rings

Wrap 4

Sl 4 sts to cn, wrap yarn counterclockwise once around these 4 sts, then k4 from cn.

Dec 6

Sl 4 wyif, *pass 2nd st on RH needle over the center st, sl center st back to LH needle and pass 2nd st on LH needle over it, sl center st back to RH needle; rep from * twice more. Pick up yarn and k center st.

Inc 2

K1 tbl in the row below next st, but do not drop from LH needle, k1, k1 tbl in same st.

▶ Cast on 38 sts.

Rows 1 and 3 (WS) P1, k5, p4, k2, [p1, k1] 4 times, p1, k2, p4, k5, p1, k5.

Row 2 K5, k1 tbl, p5, wrap 4, p2, [k1, p1] 4 times, k1, p2, wrap 4, p5, k1 tbl.

Row 4 K5, k1 tbl, p4, 1/1 RPC, 3/1 LPC, p1, [k1, p1] 5 times, 1/3 RPC, 1/1 LPC, p4, k1 tbl.

Row 5 P1, k4, p1, k2, p3, [k1, p1] 5 times, k1, p3, k2, p1, k4, p1, k5.

Row 6 K5, k1 tbl, p3, 1/1 RPC, p2, 3/2 LPC, [p1, k1] 3 times, p1, 2/3 RPC, p2, 1/1 LPC, p3, k1 tbl.

Row 7 P1, k3, p1, k5, p3, [k1, p1] 3 times, k1, p3, k5, p1, k3, p1, k5.

Row 8 K5, k1 tbl, p2, 1/1 RPC, p5, 3/3 LPC, k1, 3/3 RPC, p5, 1/1 LPC, p2, k1 tbl.

Row 9 P1, k2, p1, k9, dec 6, k9, p1, k2, p1, k5.

Row 10 K5, k1 tbl, p2, k1, p9, M1, inc 2, M1, p9, k1, p2, k1 tbl.

Row 11 P1, k2, p1, k9, p2, [p1, yo, p1] in next st, p2, k9, p1, k2, p1, k5.

Row 12 K5, k1 tbl, p2, 1/1 LPC, p5, 3/3 RPC, k1 tbl, 3/3 LPC, p5, 1/1 RPC, p2, k1.

Row 13 P1, k3, p1, k5, p3, [k1, p1] 3 times, k1, p3, k5, p1, k3, p1, k5.

Row 14 K5, k1 tbl, p3, 1/1 LPC, p2, 2/3 RPC, p1, [k1, p1] 3 times, 3/2 LPC, p2, 1/1 RPC, p3, k1 tbl.

Row 15 P1, k4, p1, k2, p3, [k1, p1] 5 times, k1, p3, k2, p1, k4, p1, k5.

Row 16 K5, k1 tbl, p4, 1/1 LPC, 3/1 RPC, [p1, k1] 5 times, p1, 3/1 LPC, 1/1 RPC, p4, k1 tbl.

Rep rows 1 to 16 until desired length, end with a RS row.

Next row (WS) Bind off 32 sts, fasten off 33rd st.

Sl rem 5 sts off needle and unravel them on every row for fringe. Cut loops and trim.

ringlets

▶ Cast on 26 sts.

Rows 1 and 3 (WS) P1 tbl, k6, p8, k11.

Row 2 K5, p6, 4-st RC, 4-st LC, p6, k1 tbl.

Row 4 K5, p4, 2/2 RPC, k4, 2/2 LPC, p4, k1 tbl.

Row 5 P1 tbl, k4, p2, k2, p4, k2, p2, k9.

Row 6 K5, p2, 2/2 RPC twice, 2/2 LPC twice, p2, k1 tbl.

Row 7 P1 tbl, [k2, p2] twice, k4, [p2, k2] twice, k5.

Row 8 K5, [p2, k2] twice, p4, [k2, p2] twice, k1 tbl.

Row 9 P1 tbl, [k2, p2] twice, k4, [p2, k2] twice, k5.

Row 10 K5, p2, 2/2 LPC twice, 2/2 RPC twice, p2, k1 tbl.

Row 11 P1 tbl, k4, p2, k2, p4, k2, p2, k9.

Row 12 K5, p4, 2/2 LPC, k4, 2/2 RPC, p4, k1 tbl.

Rep rows 1 to 12 until desired length, end with a RS row.

Bind off 20 sts, fasten off st 21.

Sl rem 5 sts off needle and unravel them on every row for fringe.

ringlets/twisted fringe

Work as for Ringlets.

Twisted fringe

Place a long tapestry needle at base of fringe loop and twist the needle clockwise until the loop kinks, then steam lightly. (Note: This works best with wool yarn.)

spliced oval

▶ Cast on 31 sts.

Row 1 (RS) K5, k1 tbl, p3, k4, p10, k4, p3, k1 tbl.

Rows 2, 4 and 6 P1, k3, p4, k10, p4, k3, p1, k5.

Row 3 K5, k1 tbl, p3, 4-st RC, p10, 4-st RC, p3, k1 tbl.

Row 5 Rep row 1.

Row 7 K5, k1 tbl, p3, 4/1 LPC, p8, 4/1 RPC, p3, k1 tbl.

Rows 8 and 26 P1, k4, p4, k8, p4, k4, p1, k5.

Row 9 K5, k1 tbl, p4, k2, 2/2 LPC, p4, 2/2 RPC, k2, p4, k1 tbl.

Rows 10 and 24 P1, k4, p2, k2, p2, k4, p2, k2, p2, k4, p1, k5.

Row 11 K5, k1b, p4, 2/2 LPC twice, 2/2 RPC twice, p4, k1 tbl.

Rows 12 and 22 P1, k6, p2, k2, p4, k2, p2, k6, p1, k5.

Row 13 K5, k1 tbl, p6, 2/2 LPC, 4-st LC, 2/2 RPC, p6, k1 tbl.

Rows 14, 16, 18 and 20 P1, k8, p8, k8, p1, k5.

Rows 15 and 19 K5, k1 tbl, p8, 4-st RC twice, p8, k1 tbl.

Row 17 K5, k1 tbl, p8, k2, 4-st LC, k2, p8, k1 tbl.

Row 21 K5, k1 tbl, p6, 2/2 RPC, 4-st LC, 2/2 LPC, p6, k1 tbl.

Row 23 K5, k1 tbl, p4, 2/2 RPC twice, 2/2 LPC twice, p4, k1 tbl.

Row 25 K5, k1 tbl, p4, k2, 2/2 RPC, p4, 2/2 LPC, k2, p4, k1 tbl.

Row 27 K5, k1 tbl, p3, 4/1 RPC, p8, 4/1 LPC, p3, k1 tbl.

Row 28 Rep row 2.

Rep rows 1 to 28 until desired length, end with a RS row.

Bind off 25 sts, fasten off 26th st.

Sl rem 5 sts off needle and unravel them on every row for fringe.

Cut loops and trim.

cable wave

▶ Cast on 19 sts.

Row 1 and all WS rows K2, p10, k7.

Row 2 K5, p2, k6, 4-st RC, p2.

Row 4 K5, p2, 4-st LC, k6, p2.

Row 6 K5, p2, k2, 4-st LC, 4-st RC, p2.

Row 8 K5, p2, 4-st LC twice, k2, p2.

Row 10 K5, p2, k6, 4-st LC, p2.

Row 12 K5, p2, 4-st LC, k6, p2.

Row 14 K5, p2, k6, 4-st RC, p2.

Row 16 K5, p2, 4-st LC, 4-st RC, k2, p2.

Row 18 K5, p2, k2, 4-st RC twice, p2.

Row 20 K5, p2, 4-st RC, k6, p2.

Rep rows 1 to 20 until desired length, end with a RS row.

Bind off 13 sts, fasten off 14th st.

Sl rem 5 sts off needle and unravel them on every row for fringe.

Cut loops and trim.

embossed wave

▶ Cast on 15 sts.

Row 1 (RS) K5, k1 tbl, p1, k2, p5, k1 tbl.

Row 2 P1, k5, p2, inc 1, p1, k5.

Row 3 K5, k1 tbl, p2, k1, ssk, p4, k1 tbl.

Row 4 P1, k4, p2, inc 1, k1, p1, k5.

Row 5 K5, k1 tbl, p3, k1, ssk, p3, k1 tbl.

Row 6 P1, k3, p2, inc 1, k2, p1, k5.

Row 7 K5, k1 tbl, p4, k1, ssk, p2, k1 tbl.

Row 8 P1, k2, p2, inc 1, k3, p1, k5.

Row 9 K5, k1 tbl, p5, k1, ssk, p1, k1 tbl.

Row 10 P1, k1, p2, k5, p1, k5.

Row 11 K5, p1 tbl, p5, k2, p1, k1 tbl.

Row 12 P1, inc 1, p2, k5, p1, k5.

Row 13 K5, k1 tbl, p4, k2tog, k1, p2, k1 tbl.

Row 14 P1, k1, inc 1, p2, k4, p1, k5.

Row 15 K5, k1 tbl, p3, k2tog, k1, p3, k1 tbl.

Row 16 P1, k2, inc 1, p2, k3, p1, k5.

Row 17 K5, k1 tbl, p2, k2tog, k1, p4, k1 tbl.

Row 18 P1, k3, inc 1, p2, k2, p1, k5.

Row 19 K5, k1 tbl, p1, k2tog, k1, p5, k1 tbl.

Row 20 P1, k5, p2, k1, p1, k5.

Rep rows 1 to 20 until desired length, end with a RS row.

Bind off 9 sts, fasten off 10th st.

Sl rem 5 sts off needle and unravel them on every row for fringe.

Cut loops and trim.

double ribbon fringe

▶ Cast on 18 sts.

Row 1 and all WS rows K5, p8, k5.

Row 2 P5, 4-st RC, 4-st LC, p5.

Row 4 P5, k8, p5.

Row 6 P5, 4-st LC, 4-st RC, p5.

Row 8 Rep row 4.

Rep rows 1 to 8 until desired length, end with row 7.

Next row P5, bind off 7 sts, fasten off 8th st.

Sl rem 5 sts each side off needle and unravel them on every row for fringe.

Cut loops and trim.

plaited fringe

▶ Cast on 18 sts.

Rows 1 and 3 (WS) K2, p8, k2, p6.
Row 2 K6, p2, 4-st RC twice, p2.
Row 4 K6, p2, k2, 4-st LC, k2, p2.
Rep rows 1 to 4 until desired
length, end with a RS row.
Bind off 12 sts, fasten off 13th st.
Sl rem 5 sts off needle and unravel
them on every row for fringe.
Cut loops and trim.

chain links

▶ Cast on 24 sts.

Prep row (WS) P1 tbl, [k2, p2 tbl] 4 times, k7.
Rows 1, 3, 5 and 7 K5, [p2, k2 tbl] 4 times, p2, k1 tbl.
Rows 2, 4, 6 and 8 P1 tbl, [k2, p2 tbl] 4 times, k7.
Row 9 K5, [p2, sl 2 to cn and hold to front, p1, k2 tbl from cn,
sl 1 to cn and hold to back, k2 tbl, p1 from cn] twice, p2, k1 tbl.
Row 10 P1 tbl, [k3, p4 tbl, k1] twice, k7.
Row 11 K5, p3, *sl 2 to cn and hold to back, k2 tbl, k2 tbl
from cn*, p4, rep between *'s once, p3, k1 tbl.
Row 12 P1 tbl, k3, p4 tbl, k4, p4 tbl, k8.
Row 13 K5, [p2, sl 1 to cn and hold to back, k2 tbl, p1 from cn,
sl 2 to cn and hold to front, p1, k2 tbl from cn] twice, p2, k1 tbl.
Row 14 P1 tbl, [k2, p2 tbl] 4 times, k7.
Rows 15 to 22 Rep rows 1 to 8.
Rep rows 1 to 22 until desired length, end with a RS row.
Bind off 18 sts, fasten off 19th st.
Sl rem 5 sts off needle and unravel them on every row for
fringe.
Cut loops and trim.

autumnal leaf

▶ Cast on 13 sts.

Prep row (WS) [K5, p1] twice, k1.
Row 1 P1, k1 tbl, p2, [(k1, k1 tbl, yo) twice, k1,
k1 tbl] in same st, p2, k1 tbl, k5—20 sts.
Row 2 K5, p1 tbl, k2, p8, k2, p1 tbl, k1.
Row 3 P1, k1 tbl, p2, k6, k2tog, p2, k1 tbl, k5.
Row 4 K5, p1 tbl, k2, p7, k2, p1 tbl, k1.
Row 5 P1, k1 tbl, p2, k5, k2tog, p2, k1 tbl, k5.
Row 6 K5, p1 tbl, k2, p6, k2, p1 tbl, k1.
Row 7 P1, k1 tbl, p2, k4, k2tog, p2, k1 tbl, k5.
Row 8 K5, p1 tbl, k2, p5, k2, p1 tbl, k1.
Row 9 P1, k1 tbl, p2, k3, k2tog, p2, k1 tbl, k5.
Row 10 K5, p1 tbl, k2, p4, k2, p1 tbl, k1.
Row 11 P1, k1 tbl, p2, k2, k2tog, p2, k1 tbl, k5.
Row 12 K5, p1 tbl, k2, p3, k2, p1 tbl, k1.
Row 13 P1, k1 tbl, p2, k1, k2tog, p2, k1 tbl, k5.
Row 14 K5, p1 tbl, k2, p2, k2, p1 tbl, k1.
Row 15 P1, k1 tbl, p2, k2tog, p2, k1 tbl, k5—13 sts.
Row 16 K5, p1 tbl, k2, p1, k2, p1 tbl, k1.
Rep rows 1 to 16 until desired length, end
with a RS row.
Bind off 7 sts, fasten off 8th st.
Sl rem 5 sts off needle and unravel them on
every row for fringe.
Cut loops and trim.

imperial bead fringe

- String 17 beads onto yarn for each pat rep of rows 1 to 32.
- Slip all sts knitwise.
▶ Cast on 12 sts

Row 1 (WS) Sl 1, k11, turn.

Row 2 SB1, k7, yo, k1, [yo, k2tog] twice.

Row 3 Sl 1, k3, p1, k8.

Row 4 SB1, k7, yo, k2, [yo, k2tog] twice.

Row 5 Sl 1, k3, p2, k8.

Row 6 SB1, k7 yo, k3, [yo, k2tog] twice.

Row 7 Sl 1, k3, p3, k8.

Row 8 SB1, k7, yo, k4, [yo, k2tog] twice.

Row 9 Sl 1, k3, p4, k8.

Row 10 SB1, k7, yo, k5, [yo, k2tog] twice.

Row 11 Sl 1, k3, p5, k8.

Row 12 SB1, k7, yo, k6, [yo, k2tog] twice.

Row 13 Sl 1, k3, p6, k8.

Row 14 SB1, k7, yo, k7, [yo, k2tog] twice.

Row 15 Sl 1, k3, p7, k8.

Row 16 SB1, k7, yo, k8, [yo, k2tog] twice—20 sts.

Row 17 Sl 1, k3, p8, k8.

Row 18 SB1, k7, yo, k2tog, k7, [yo, k2tog] twice.

Row 19 Sl 1, k3, p6, p2tog, k8.

Row 20 SB1, k7, yo, k2tog, k6, [yo, k2tog] twice.

Row 21 Sl 1, k3, p5, p2tog, k8.

Row 22 SB1, k7, yo, k2tog, k5, [yo, k2tog] twice.

Row 23 Sl 1, k3, p4, p2tog, k8.

Row 24 SB1, k7, yo, k2tog, k4, [yo, k2tog] twice.

Row 25 Sl 1, k3, p3, p2tog, k8.

Row 26 SB1, k7, yo, k2tog, k3, [yo, k2tog] twice.

Row 27 Sl 1, k3, p2, p2tog, k8.

Row 28 SB1, k7, yo, k2tog, k2, [yo, k2tog] twice.

Row 29 Sl 1, k3, p1, p2tog, k8.

Row 30 SB1, k7, k2tog, k1, [yo, k2tog] twice.

Row 31 Sl 1, k3, p2tog, k7—12 sts.

Row 32 SB1, k7, k1, [yo, k2tog] twice.

Rep rows 1 to 32 until desired length, end with a RS row.

Bind off 5 sts, fasten off 6th st.

Sl rem 6 sts off needle and unravel them on every row for fringe.

Sew additional beads to St st areas.

beaded loop fringe

▲ (multiple of 2 sts)

- Thread beads onto yarn.

Note: Make sure that yarn and needle will fit through bead hole.

Row 1 (WS) Purl.

Row 2 Knit.

Row 3 P1, *sl 3"/7.5cm of beads close to RH needle, k1 tbl, k1; rep from *, end p1.

Rows 4 and 6 Knit.

Rows 5 and 7 Purl.

Rep rows 2 to 7 for each layer of beaded fringe desired.

Cont as desired.

double loop stitch

▲ (multiple of 2 sts plus 1)

• The loops in this edging are formed on the RS but are worked on a WS row.

Rows 1, 2 and 3 Knit.

Row 4 (WS) K1, *insert RH needle into next st as if to knit it, wind yarn over RH needle and around first and second fingers of left hand twice, then over RH needle point once more, draw all 3 loops through st and sl on to LH needle, insert RH needle through back of these 3 loops and original st and k them tog tbl, k1; rep from * to end.

Rows 5, 6, and 7 Knit.

Row 8 K1, *k1, insert RH needle into next st on as if to knit it, wind yarn over RH needle and around first and second fingers of left hand twice, then over RH needle point once more, draw all 3 loops through st and sl on to LH needle, insert RH needle through back of these 3 loops and original st and k them tog tbl; rep from *, end k2.

Rep rows 1 to 8 until desired length.

Cont as desired.

chain loop stitch

▲ (multiple of 2 sts 1)

• A crochet hook is used to form the loops in this edging. The density of the edging can be changed by the position of each chain loop on the background and by the number of rows worked between each pat row.

Prep row (WS) Knit.

Row 1 K1, *k next st and leave on LH needle, insert crochet hook from front to back through lp on LH needle, draw a lp through and on to hook, then drop st from LH needle, ch 12, wyib and ch in front, sl lp to RH needle and remove hook, then lift last st over lp (L1), k1; rep from * to end.

Rows 2 and 4 Purl.

Row 3 K1, *k1, L1; rep from *, end k2.

Rep rows 1 to 4 until desired length.

Cont as desired.

faux fur

▲ (multiple of 2 sts plus 1)

• The loops in this edging are formed on the RS but are worked on a WS row. The loop is formed by wrapping the yarn around one or more fingers, depending on the length of loops desired.

Rows 1 and 3 (RS) Knit.

Row 2 K1, *ML, k1; rep from * to end.

Row 4 K2, *ML, k1; rep from *, end last rep k2.

Rep rows 1 to 4 until desired length.

Cont as desired.

single loop stitch

▲ (multiple of 2 sts plus 1)

• The loops in this edging are formed on a RS row.

Rows 1 and 5 (RS) Knit.

Rows 2 and all WS rows Purl.

Row 3 *K1 and leave st on LH needle, wyif wrap yarn clockwise around left thumb to make a lp 1½"/4cm long, wyib k st rem on LH needle letting it drop from the needle, then return the 2 sts just worked to the LH needle and k them tog; rep from *, end k1.

Row 7 K1, *k1 and leave st on LH needle, wyif wrap yarn clockwise to make a lp 1½"/4cm long, wyib k st rem on LH needle letting it drop from the needle, then return the 2 sts just worked to the LH needle and k them tog; rep from *, end k2.

Row 8 Purl.

Rep rows 1 to 8 until desired length.

Cont as desired.

loop stitch

▲ (multiple of 2 sts plus 1)

• Yarn is wrapped around the left thumb to form loops.

Row 1 (RS) K1, *[k1 and leave st on LH needle, wyif, wrap yarn clockwise once around left thumb to make loop, wyib, k into back of same st], k1; rep from *.

Row 2 P1, *p2tog, p1; rep from * to end.

Row 3 K2, *[k1 and leave st on LH needle, wyif, wrap yarn clockwise once around left thumb to make loop, wyib, k into back of same st]; rep from *, end last rep k2.

Row 4 P2, *p2tog, p1; rep from *, end last rep p2.

Rep rows 1 to 4 until desired length.

Cont as desired.

fur yarn

With "fur" yarn, cast on number of sts needed.

K until desired length.

Change to MC and cont as desired.

sassy fringe

▶ Using a single cast on, *cast on 9 sts.
Bind off 8 sts. Place rem lp on LH needle.
Rep from * until desired width.
Fasten off.
For shorter fringe: cast on fewer sts.
For longer fringe: cast on more sts.

friseur fringe

▶ Cast on 23 sts.
Rows 1, 2, 5 and 6 Knit.
Rows 3 and 7 Bind off 19 sts, k to end—4 sts.
Row 4 K4, using the cable cast-on method, cast on 19 sts.
Rep rows 4 to 7 until desired length, end with row 6.
Bind off.

corkscrew fringe

▲ (Cast on over two needles or *very* loosely–over
any number of sts)
• The fringe is knitted separately and then attached. The yarn
weight and number of sts cast on will determine the length.
Loosely cast on any number of sts.
Row 1 K into the front, back and front again of each st across.
Row 2 Bind off purlwise.
Use fingers to twist each tassel into a corkscrew.

curly cue trim

Cast on number of sts needed for edge. On
spare needle, work corkscrew fringe (see
above) long enough to fit along edge. With
spare needle, pick up st on each twist. With
both needles parallel, *k corkscrew and cast-on
st tog, k3 cast-on sts; rep from *, end k
corkscrew and cast-on st tog.
Cont as desired.

gossamer tassel

(multiple of 2 sts plus 1)

Using the Double Cast-on Method, cast on 37 sts.

Work rows 1 and 2 of Gossamer Fringe Ruffle (see page 62) for 3"/7.5 cm, end with a WS row.

Next row (RS) K1 tbl, *sl next st off needle and allow it to drop to cast on edge, p1, k1 tbl; rep from * to end—25 sts.

Row 1 P1, *k1 tbl, p1; rep from * to end.

Row 2 K1 tbl, *p1, k1 tbl; rep from * to end.

Rep rows 1 and 2 five times more (12 rows).

Cut yarn, leaving a long end and pull through rem sts and draw up tightly to secure. Insert a 1"/2.5cm styrofoam ball into top of tassel or stuff with fiberfill. Sew back seam.

Wrap yarn around base of ball. Make tie and secure to top.

basic tassel

Wrap yarn around a piece of cardboard 4"/10cm wide by desired length of tassel plus 1"/2.5cm for tying and trimming. Wrap yarn 40 times (or to desired thickness) around length of cardboard. Insert a strand of yarn through cardboard and tie it at the top.

Cut the lower edge. Wrap a 12"/30.5cm piece of yarn 1½"/4cm below top knot to form tassel neck. Trim ends even.

basic tassel with knitted band

Make Basic Tassel but do not tie neck.

Band

With CC, cast on number of sts needed to fit around tassel neck. K 2 rows. Bind off.

Wrap band 1"/2.5cm down from top. Sew cast-on edge to bound-off edge.

perfect pompom

Follow pompom directions on page 166. Make Corkscrew Fringe (see page 110) and sew to pompom.

garter stitch tassel

With A and B held tog, cast on 16 sts.

Work as for Garter Stitch Fringe (see page 99) for 2¾"/6.5cm, end with a RS row.

Bind off 9 sts, fasten off 10th st. Sl rem 6 sts off needle and unravel them on every row for fringe.

Weave yarn in and out of every other st along side edge and pull closed. Insert 1"/2.5cm styrofoam ball into tassel and sew back seam.

Band

With A and B held tog, cast on 10 sts. K 1 row. Bind off. Sew band around neck.

corkscrew tassel trio

Make 3 Corkscrew Fringes (see page 110) each a different length. Sew tog at one end.

113

flora

layered leaves/berries

MB [K1, p1] twice in next st—4 sts, turn, p4, turn, k4, turn, p4, turn, [k2tog] twice, turn, p2tog.

▲ (multiple of 6 sts plus 5)

• On WS rows, purl the yo tbl.

Row 1 (RS) *P5, MB; rep from *, end p5.

Row 2 *K5, p1; rep from *, end k5.

Row 3 *P5, yo, k1; rep from *, end p5.

Rows 4 and 12 K5 *p2, k5; rep from * to end.

Row 5 *P5, yo, k2; rep from *, end p5.

Rows 6 and 10 K5, *p3, k5; rep from * to end.

Row 7 *P5, yo, k3; rep from *, end p5.

Row 8 K5, *p4, k5; rep from * to end.

Row 9 *P5, k2, k2tog; rep from *, end p5.

Row 11 *P5, k1, k2tog; rep from *, end p5.

Row 13 *P5, k2tog; rep from *, end p5.

Row 14 K5 *p1, k5; rep from * to end.

Row 15 *P2, yo, k1, p3; rep from *, end p2, yo, k1, p2.

Row 16 K2, p2, k2, *k3, p2, k2; rep from * to end.

Row 17 *P2, yo, k2, p3; rep from *, end p2, yo, k2, p2.

Row 18 K2, p3, k2, *k3, p3, k2; rep from * to end.

Row 19 *P2, yo, k3, p3; rep from *, end p2, yo, k3, p2.

Row 20 K2, p4, k2, *k3, p4, k2; rep from * to end.

Row 21 *P2, k2, k2tog, p3; rep from *, end p2, k2, k2tog, p2.

Row 22 K2, p3, k2, *k3, p3, k2; rep from * to end.

Row 23 *P2, k1, k2tog, p3; rep from *, end p2, k1, k2tog, p2.

Row 24 K2, p2, k2, *k3, p2, k2; rep from * to end.

Row 25 *P2, k2tog, p3; rep from *, end p2, k2tog, p2.

Row 26 K2, p1, k2, *k3, p1, k2; rep from * to end.

Rows 27 and 29 Knit.

Rows 28 and 30 Purl.

Cont as desired.

tulip bud

▲ (multiple of 37 sts)

Row 1 (WS) *K18, p1, k18; rep from * to end.

Row 2 *K16, k2tog, yo, k1, yo, ssk, k16; rep from * to end.

Row 3 *K16, p5, k16; rep from * to end.

Row 4 *K15, k2tog, yo, k3, yo, ssk, k15; rep from * to end.

Row 5 *K15, p7, k15; rep from * to end.

Row 6 *K14, [k2tog, yo] twice, k1, [yo, ssk] twice, k14; rep from * to end.

Row 7 *K14, p9, k14; rep from * to end.

Row 8 *K13, [k2tog, yo] twice, k3, [yo, ssk] twice, k13; rep from * to end.

Row 9 *K13, p4, k1, p1, k1, p4, k13; rep from * to end.

Row 10 *K12, [k2tog, yo] twice, k5, [yo, ssk] twice, k12; rep from * to end.

Row 11 *K12, p4, k2, p1, k2, p4, k12; rep from * to end.

Row 12 *K11, [k2tog, yo] twice, k3, yo, k1, yo, k3, [yo, ssk] twice, k11; rep from * to end—39 sts.

Row 13 *K11, p4, k3, p3, k3, p4, k11; rep from * to end.

Row 14 *K3, yo, ssk, k5, [k2tog, yo] twice, k5, yo, k1, yo, k5, [yo, ssk] twice, k5, k2tog, yo, k3; rep from * to end—41 sts.

Row 15 *K3, p2, k5, p4, k4, p5, k4, p4, k5, p2, k3; rep from * to end.

Row 16 *K4, yo, ssk, k3, [k2tog, yo] twice, k7, yo, k1, yo, k7, [yo, ssk] twice, k3, k2tog, yo, k4; rep from * to end—43 sts.

Row 17 *K4, p2, k3, p4, k5, p7, k5, p4, k3, p2, k4; rep from * to end.

Row 18 *K5, yo, ssk, k1, [k2tog, yo] twice, k9, yo, k1, yo, k9, [yo, ssk] twice, k1, k2tog, yo, k5; rep from * to end—45 sts.

Row 19 *K5, p2, k1, p4, k6, p9, k6, p4, k1, p2, k5; rep from * to end.

Row 20 *K6, yo, SK2P, yo, k2tog, yo, k7, ssk, k5, k2tog, k7, yo, ssk, yo, k3tog, yo, k6; rep from * to end—43 sts.

Row 21 *K6, p5, k7, p7, k7, p5, k6; rep from * to end.

Row 22 *K18, ssk, k3, k2tog, k18; rep from * to end—41 sts.

Row 23 *K18, p5, k18; rep from * to end.

Row 24 *K18, ssk, k1, k2tog, k18; rep from * to end—39 sts.

Row 25 *K18, p3, k18; rep from * to end.

Row 26 *K18, SK2P, k18; rep from * to end—37 sts.

Cont as desired.

windblown leaf border

▲ (multiple of 6 sts plus 5)

Rows 1, 3 and 5 (WS) K7, *k1, p1 tbl, k4; rep from *, end last rep k2.

Rows 2 and 4 P2, k1 tbl, p1, *p4, k1 tbl, p1; rep from *, end p7.

Row 6 P2, [k1, yo, k1] in next st, p1, *p4, [k1, yo, k1] in next st, p1; rep from *, end p7.

Row 7 K7, *k1, p3, k4; rep from *, end last rep k2.

Row 8 P1, inc 1 p-st, [k1, yo] twice, k1, *p2tog, p2, inc 1 p-st, [k1, yo] twice, k1; rep from *, end p2tog, p6.

Row 9 K7, *p5, k5; rep from *, end last rep k3.

Row 10 P2, inc 1 p-st, k2, yo, k1, yo, k2, *p2tog, p2, inc 1 p-st, k2, yo, k1, yo, k2; rep from *, end p2tog, p5.

Row 11 K6, p7, *k5, p7; rep from *, end k4.

Row 12 P3, inc 1 p-st, *k3, yo, k1, yo, k3, p2tog, p2, inc 1 p-st; rep from *, end last rep p4.

Row 13 K5, p9, k1, *k4, p9, k1; rep from *, end k4.

Row 14 P4, *inc 1 p-st, ssk, k5, k2tog, p2tog, p2; rep from *, end last rep p3.

Row 15 K4, p7, k2, *k3, p7, k2; rep from *, end k4.

Row 16 P4, *p1, inc 1 p-st, ssk, k3, k2tog, p2tog, p1; rep from *, end last rep p2.

Row 17 K3, p5, k3, *k2, p5, k3; rep from *, end k4.

Row 18 P4, *p2, inc 1 p-st, ssk, k1, k2tog, p2tog; rep from * end p1.

Row 19 K2, p3, k4, *k1, p3, k4; rep from *, end k4.

Row 20 P4, *p4, SK2P, p1; rep from *, end last rep p2.

Row 21 Knit.

Row 22 Purl.

Cont as desired.

leaf fringe

▼ I-cord ◄►

With dpn, cast on 3 sts. K3, *do not turn work. Slide sts to beg of dpn and k3; rep from * for I-cord until piece measures 1"/2.5cm, inc 1 st each side on next row—5 sts.

Leaf

Row 1 (RS) K2, yo, k1, yo, k2.

Row 2 and all WS rows Purl.

Row 3 K3, yo, k1, yo, k3.

Row 5 K4, yo, k1, yo, k4—11 sts.

Row 7 Ssk, k7, k2tog.

Row 9 Ssk, k5, k2tog.

Row 11 Ssk, k3, k2tog.

Row 13 Ssk, k1, k2tog.

Row 15 SK2P.

Fasten off.

Leaf back

Cast on 5 sts and work rows 1 to 15 of Leaf.

With WS tog, sew leaf back to leaf.

embossed leaf stitch

▲ (multiple of 7 sts plus 6)

K 2 rows.

Row 1 (RS) P6, *yo, k1, yo, p6; rep from * to end.

Rows 2 and 14 *K6, p3; rep from *, end k6.

Row 3 P6, *k1, yo, k1, yo, k1, p6; rep from * to end.

Rows 4 and 12 *K6, p5; rep from *, end k6.

Row 5 P6 *k2, yo, k1, yo, k2, p6; rep from * to end.

Rows 6 and 10 *K6, p7; rep from *, end k6.

Row 7 P6, *k3, yo, k1, yo, k3, p6; rep from * to end.

Row 8 *K6, p9 ; rep from *, end k6.

Row 9 P6, *SKP, k5, k2tog, p6; rep from * to end.

Row 11 P6, *SKP, k3, k2tog, p6; rep from * to end.

Row 13 P6, *SKP, k1, k2tog, p6; rep from * to end.

Row 15 P6, *SK2P, p6; rep from * to end.

Row 16 Knit.

Cont as desired.

Make **Bobbles** (see page 164) and sew to bottom of leaf.

leaf points

▲ (beg as a multiple of 2 sts and end as a multiple of 29 sts)

• Each point is worked separately, then all points are joined on the same row.

Cast on 2 sts.

Row 1 (RS) Yo, k2.

Row 2 Yo, k1, p1, k1.

Row 3 Yo, [k1, yo] twice, k2.

Row 4 Yo, k2, p3, k2.

Row 5 Yo, k1, p1, k1, [yo, k1] twice, p3.

Row 6 Yo, k3, p5, k3.

Row 7 Yo, k1, p2, k2, yo, k1, yo, k2, p4.

Row 8 Yo, k4, p7, k4.

Row 9 Yo, k1, p3, k3, yo, k1, yo, k3, p5.

Row 10 Yo, k5, p9, k5.

Row 11 Yo, k1, p4, k4, yo, k1, yo, k4, p6.

Row 12 Yo, k6, p11, k6.

Row 13 Yo, k1, p5, k5, yo, k1, yo, k5, p7.

Row 14 Yo, k7, p13, k7.

Row 15 Yo, k1, p6, SKP, k9, k2tog, p8.

Row 16 Yo, k8, p11, k8.

Row 17 Yo, k1, p7, SKP, k7, k2tog, p9.

Row 18 Yo, k9, p9, k9.

Row 19 Yo, k1, p8, SKP, k5, k2tog, p10.

Row 20 Yo, k10, p7, k10.

Row 21 Yo, k1, p9, SKP, k3, k2tog, p11.

Row 22 Yo, k11, p5, k11.

Row 23 Yo, k1, p10, SKP, k1, k2tog, p12.

Row 24 Yo, k12, p3, k12.

Row 25 Yo, k1, p11, SK2P, p13.

Row 26 Yo, k27.

Row 27 Yo, k1, p27—29 sts.

Break yarn and leave sts on needle.

On same needle, cast on and work rows 1 to 27 to make another point. Cont in this manner until desired number of points are made. Turn and work across all points on needle to join.

Cont as desired.

Make **Bobbles** (see page 164) and sew to each point.

scalloped leaves

▶ Cast on 8 sts.

Row 1 (RS) K5, yo, k1, yo, k2.

Row 2 P6, inc 1, k3.

Row 3 K4, p1, k2, yo, k1, yo, k3.

Row 4 P8, inc 1, k4.

Row 5 K4, p2, k3, yo, k1, yo, k4.

Row 6 P10, inc 1, k5.

Row 7 K4, p3, k4, yo, k1, yo, k5.

Row 8 P12, inc 1, k6—20 sts.

Row 9 K4, p4, ssk, k7, k2tog, k1.

Row 10 P10, inc 1, k7.

Row 11 K4, p5, ssk, k5, k2tog, k1.

Row 12 P8, inc 1, k2, p1, k5.

Row 13 K4, p1, k1, p4, ssk, k3, k2tog, k1.

Row 14 P6, inc 1, k3, p1, k5.

Row 15 K4, p1, k1, p5, ssk, k1, k2tog, k1.

Row 16 P4, inc 1, k4, p1, k5.

Row 17 K4, p1, k1, p6, SK2P, k1.

Row 18 P2tog, bind off 5 sts, p3, k4—8 sts.

Rep rows 1 to 18 until desired length.

Bind off.

raised leaf insert (horizontal)

▶ Cast on 21 sts.

K 4 rows.

Rows 1 and 3 (RS) K2, p8, k1, p8, k2.

Rows 2 and 4 K10, p1, k10.

Row 5 K2, p8, yo, k1, yo, p8, k2.

Rows 6 and 18 K10, p3, k10.

Row 7 K2, p8, [k1, yo] twice, k1, p8, k2.

Rows 8 and 16 K10, p5, k10.

Row 9 K2, p8, k2, [yo, k1] twice, k1, p8, k2.

Rows 10 and 14 K10, p7, k10.

Row 11 K2, p8, k3, yo, k1, yo, k3, p8, k2—29 sts.

Row 12 K10, p9, k10.

Row 13 K2, p8, k3, SK2P, k3, p8, k2.

Row 15 K2, p8, k2, SK2P, k2, p8, k2.

Row 17 K2, p8, k1, SK2P, k1, p8, k2.

Row 19 K2, p8, SK2P, p8, k2—21 sts.

Row 20 Rep row 2.

Rep rows 1 to 20 until desired length.

Bind off.

embossed twining vine leaf

▶ Cast on 26 sts.

Row 1 (WS) K5, p5, k4, p3, k9.

Row 2 P7, p2tog, inc 1, k2, p4, k2, yo, k1, yo, k2, p5.

Row 3 K5, p7, k4, p2, k1, p1, k8.

Row 4 P6, p2tog, k1, inc 1 p-st, k2, p4, k3, yo, k1, yo, k3, p5.

Row 5 K5, p9, k4, p2, k2, p1, k7.

Row 6 P5, p2tog, k1, inc 1 p-st, p1, k2, p4, ssk, k5, k2tog, p5.

Row 7 K5, p7, k4, p2, k3, p1, k6.

Row 8 P4, p2tog, k1, inc 1 p-st, p2, k2, p4, ssk, k3, k2tog, p5.

Row 9 K5, p5, k4, p2, k4, p1, k5.

Row 10 P5, yo, k1, yo, p4, k2, p4, ssk, k1, k2tog, p5.

Row 11 K5, p3, k4, p2, k4, p3, k5.

Row 12 P5, [k1, yo] twice, k1, p4, k1, M1, k1, p2tog, p2, SK2P, p5.

Row 13 K9, p3, k4, p5, k5.

Row 14 P5, k2, yo, k1, yo, k2, p4, k1, inc 1, k1, p2tog, p7.

Row 15 K8, p1, k1, p2, k4, p7, k5.

Row 16 P5, k3, yo, k1, yo, k3, p4, k2, inc 1 p-st, k1, p2tog, p6.

Row 17 K7, p1, k2, p2, k4, p9, k5.

Row 18 P5, ssk, k5, k2tog, p4, k2, p1, inc 1 p-st, k1, p2tog, p5.

Row 19 K6, p1, k3, p2, k4, p7, k5.

Row 20 P5, ssk, k3, k2tog, p4, k2, p2, inc 1 p-st, k1, p2tog, p4.

Row 21 K5, p1, k4, p2, k4, p5, k5.

Row 22 P5, ssk, k1, k2tog, p4, k2, p4, yo, k1, yo, p5.

Row 23 K5, p3, k4, p2, k4, p3, k5.

Row 24 P5, SK2P, p2, p2tog, k1, M1, k1, p4, [k1, yo] twice, k1, p5.

Rep rows 1 to 24 until desired length.

Bind off.

loop trees

▲ (multiple of 18 sts)

Row 1 (RS) *P5, [k1 wrapping yarn twice, p1] 5 times, p3; rep from * to end.

Row 2 *K4, [sl 1 wyif letting extra wrap drop, k1] 5 times, k4; rep from * to end.

Row 3 *P5, [sl 1 wyib, p1] 5 times, p3; rep from * to end.

Row 4 *K4, [sl 1 wyif, k1] 5 times, k4; rep from * to end.

Row 5 *P5, k1, [p1, k1 wrapping yarn twice] 3 times, p1, k1, p4; rep from * to end.

Row 6 *K6, [sl 1 wyif letting extra wrap drop, k1] 3 times, k6; rep from * to end.

Row 7 *P7, [sl 1 wyib, p1] 3 times, p6; rep from * to end.

Row 8 *K6, [sl 1 wyif, k1] 3 times, k6; rep from * to end.

Row 9 *P7, k1, p1, k1 wrapping yarn twice, p1, k1, p6; rep from * to end.

Row 10 *K8, sl 1 wyif letting extra wrap drop, k9; rep from * to end.

Row 11 *P9, sl 1 wyib, p8; rep from * to end.

Work in rev St st or as desired until desired length.

Cont as desired.

falling leaves I

▲ (multiple of 14 sts plus 9)

K 2 rows.

Row 1 (RS) Sl 1, k3, SKP, k5, yo, k1, yo, *k5, SK2P, k5, yo, k1, yo; rep from *, end last rep k5, SKP, k4.

Row 2 Sl 1, k9, *p3, k11; rep from *, end last rep k10.

Row 3 Sl 1, k3, SKP, k4, yo, k3, yo, *k4, SK2P, k4, yo, k3, yo; rep from *, end last rep k4, SKP, k4.

Row 4 Sl 1, k8 *p5, k9; rep from * to end.

Row 5 Sl 1, k3, SKP, k3, yo, k5, yo, *k3, SK2P, k3, yo, k5, yo; rep from *, end last rep k3, SKP, k4.

Row 6 Sl 1 *k7, p7; rep from *, end last rep k8.

Row 7 Sl 1, k3, SKP, k2, yo, k7, yo *k2, SK2P, k2, yo, k7, yo; rep from *, end last rep k2, SKP, k4.

Row 8 Sl 1, k6, *p9, k5; rep from *, end last rep k7.

Row 9 Sl 1, k3, SKP, k1, yo, k9, yo, *k1, SK2P, k1, yo, k9, yo; rep from *, end last rep k1, SKP, k4.

Row 10 Sl 1, k5, *p11, k3; rep from *, end last rep k6.

Row 11 Sl 1, k3, SKP, yo, k11, yo, *SK2P, yo, k11, yo; rep from *, end last rep SKP, k4.

Row 12 Sl 1, k4, *p13, k1; rep from *, end last rep k5.

Row 13 Sl 1, k4, *yo, k5, SK2P, k5, yo, k1; rep from *, end last rep k5.

Row 14 Rep row 10.

Row 15 Sl 1, k5, *yo, k4, SK2P, k4, yo, k3; rep from *, end last rep k6.

Row 16 Rep row 8.

Row 17 Sl 1, k6, *yo, k3, SK2P, k3, yo, k5; rep from *, end last rep k7.

Row 18 Rep row 6.

Row 19 Sl 1, *k7, yo, k2, SK2P, k2, yo; rep from *, end k8.

Row 20 Rep row 4.

Row 21 Sl 1, k8, *yo, k1, SK2P, k1, yo, k9; rep from * to end.

Row 22 Rep row 2.

Row 23 Sl 1, k9 *yo SK2P, yo, k11; rep from *, end last rep k10.

Row 24 Sl 1, k10, *p1, k13; rep from *, end last rep k11.

Cont as desired.

falling leaves II

▲ Work as for **Falling Leaves I**.

Make **Bobbles** (page 164) and sew to lower points.

royal leaf

▲ (multiple of 14 plus 1)

Row 1 (RS) K1, yo, p5, p3tog, *p5, yo, k1, yo, p5, p3tog; rep from *, end p5, yo, k1.

Row 2 and all WS rows Purl.

Rows 3 to 12 Rep rows 1 and 2 five more times.

Row 13 K1, yo, SKP, yo, p3, p3tog, *p3, yo, k2tog, yo, k1, yo, SKP, yo, p3, p3tog; rep from * end p3, yo, k2tog, yo, k1.

Row 15 K1, yo, k1, SKP, yo, p2, p3tog, *p2, yo, k2tog, (k1, yo) twice, k1, SKP, yo, p2, p3tog; rep from * end p2, yo, k2tog, k1, yo, k1.

Row 17 K1, yo, k2, SKP, yo, p1, p3tog, *p1, yo, k2tog, k2, yo, k1, yo, k2, SKP, yo, p1, p3tog; rep from *, end p1, yo, k2tog, k2, yo, k1.

Row 19 K1, yo, k3, SKP, yo, p3tog, *yo, k2tog, k3, yo, k1, yo, k3, SKP, yo, p3tog; rep from * end yo, k2tog, k3, yo, k1.

Row 21 K4, k2tog, yo, k2, *k1, yo, SKP, k7, k2tog, yo, k2; rep from *, end k1, yo, SKP, K4.

Row 23 K3, k2tog, yo, k3, *k2, yo, SKP, k5, k2tog, yo, k3; rep from *, end k2, yo, SKP, k3.

Row 25 K2, k2tog, yo, k4, *k3, yo, SKP, k3, k2tog, yo, k4; rep from *, end k3, yo, SKP, k2.

Row 27 K1, k2tog, yo, k5, *k4, yo, SKP, k1, k2tog, yo, k5; rep from * end k4, yo, SKP, k1.

Row 29 K2tog, yo, k6, *k5, yo, SK2P, yo, k6; rep from * end k5, yo, SKP.

Row 30 Purl.

Continue as desired

Make **Bobbles** (see page 164) and sew to lower points

checkered raised-leaf border

▶ Cast on 37 sts.

K 1 row.

Row 1 (RS) K3, yo, k2tog, k3, p7, k3, yo, k2tog, yo, k17—38 sts.

Row 2 K20, p3, k7, p3, k5.

Row 3 K3, yo, k2tog, k3, p7, k3, yo, k2tog, k1, yo, k17—39 sts.

Row 4 K21, p13, k5.

Row 5 K3, yo, k2tog, p3, k7, p3, [yo, k2tog] twice, yo, k8, yo, k1, yo, k8—42 sts.

Row 6 K8, p3, k16, p7, k8.

Row 7 K3, yo, k2tog, p3, k7, p3, yo, k2tog, k1, yo, k2tog, yo, k9, yo, k1, yo, k9—45 sts.

Row 8 K8, p5, k14, p13, k5.

Row 9 K3, yo, k2tog, k3, p7, k3, [yo, k2tog] 3 times, yo, k10, yo, k1, yo, k10—48 sts.

Row 10 K8, p7, k15, p3, k7, p3, k5.

Row 11 K3, yo, k2tog, k3, p7, k3, yo, k2tog, k1, [yo, k2tog] twice, yo, k11, yo, k1, yo, k11—51 sts.

Row 12 K8, p9, k16, p13, k5.

Row 13 K3, yo, k2tog, p3, k7, p3, [yo, k2tog] 4 times, yo, k12, yo, k1, yo, k12—54 sts.

Row 14 K8, p11, k20, p7, k8.

Row 15 K3, yo, k2tog, p3, k7, p3, yo, k2tog, k1, [yo, k2tog] 3 times, yo, k8, SKP, k7, k2tog, k8—53 sts.

Row 16 K8, p9, k18, p13, k5.

Row 17 K3, yo, k2tog, k3, p7, k3, [yo, k2tog] 5 times, yo, k8, SKP, k5, k2tog, k8—52 sts.

Row 18 K8, p7, k19, p3, k7, p3, k5.

Row 19 K3, yo, k2tog, k3, p7, k3, yo, k2tog, k1, [yo, k2tog] 4 times, yo, k8, SKP, k3, k2tog, k8—51 sts.

Row 20 K8, p5, k20, p13, k5.

Row 21 K3, yo, k2tog, p3, k7, p3, [yo, k2tog] 6 times, yo, k8, SKP, k1, k2tog, k8—50 sts.

Row 22 K8, p3, k24, p7, k8.

Row 23 K3, yo, k2tog, p3, k7, p3, yo, k2tog, k1, [yo, k2tog] 5 times, yo, k8, SK2P, k8—49 sts.

Row 24 K31, p13, k5.

Row 25 K3, yo, k2tog, k3, p7, k3, [yo, k2tog] 7 times, yo, k17—50 sts.

Row 26 Bind off 13 sts, k18, p3, k7, p3, k5.

Rep rows 1 to 26 until desired length.

Bind off.

fern and bobble point

▶ Cast on 21 sts.

Row 1 (RS) K2, k2tog, yo twice, k2tog twice, yo twice, k2tog, k2, yo twice, k2tog, k7.

Row 2 K9, p1, k4, [p1, k3] twice.

Row 3 K2, k2tog, yo twice, k2tog twice, yo twice, k2tog, k1, MB, k2, yo twice, k2tog, k6.

Row 4 K8, p1, k6, [p1, k3] twice.

Row 5 K2, k2tog, yo twice, k2tog twice, yo twice, k2tog, k3, MB, k2, yo twice, k2tog, k5.

Row 6 K7, p1, k8, [p1, k3] twice.

Row 7 K2, k2tog, yo twice, k2tog twice, yo twice, k2tog, k5, MB, k2, yo twice, k2tog, k4.

Row 8 K6, p1, k10, [p1, k3] twice.

Row 9 K2, k2tog, yo twice, k2tog twice, yo twice, k2tog, k7, MB, k2, yo twice, k2tog, k3.

Row 10 K5, p1, k12, [p1, k3] twice.

Row 11 K2, k2tog, yo twice, k2tog twice, yo twice, k2tog, k9, MB, k2, yo twice, k2tog, k2.

Row 12 K4, p1, k14, [p1, k3] twice.

Row 13 K2, k2tog, yo twice, k2tog twice, yo twice, k2tog, k11, MB, k2, yo twice, k2tog, k1.

Row 14 K3, p1, k16, [p1, k3] twice.

Row 15 K2, k2tog, yo twice, k2tog twice, yo twice, k2tog, k18—28 sts.

Row 16 Bind off 7 sts, k12, [p1, k3] twice—21 sts.

Rep rows 1 to 16 until desired length.

Bind off.

diamonds and leaves-horizontal

▶ Cast on 30 sts.

K 1 row.

Row 1 (RS) Sl 1, k8, k2tog, yo, k1, yo, SKP, k7, k2tog, yo twice, k1, [yo, k1] twice, yo twice, SKP, k2—34 sts.

Row 2 Sl 1, k3, p7, k8, k2tog, yo, k3, yo, SKP, k8.

Row 3 Sl 1, k6, k2tog, yo, k5, yo, SKP, k5, k2tog, yo twice, SKP, k1, [yo, k1] twice, k2tog, yo twice, SKP, k2—36 sts.

Row 4 Sl 1, k3, p9, k6, k2tog, yo, k7, yo, SKP, k6.

Row 5 Sl 1, k4, k2tog, yo, k9, yo, SKP, k3, k2tog, yo twice, SKP, k5, k2tog, yo twice, SKP, k2.

Row 6 Sl 1, k3, p9, k4, k2tog, yo, k11, yo, SKP, k4.

Row 7 Sl 1, k2, k2tog, yo, k13, yo, SKP, k1, k2tog, yo twice, SKP, k5, k2tog, yo twice, SKP, k2.

Row 8 Sl 1, k3, p1, p2tog, p3, p2tog, p1, k4, yo, SKP, k11, k2tog, yo, k4—34 sts.

Row 9 Sl 1, k4, yo, SKP, k9, k2tog, yo, k5, yo twice, SKP, k3, k2tog, yo twice, SKP, k2—35 sts.

Row 10 Sl 1, k3, [p1, p2tog] twice, p1, k7, yo, SKP, k7, k2tog, yo, k6—33 sts.

Row 11 Sl 1, k6, yo, SKP, k5, k2tog, yo, k8, yo twice, SKP, k1, k2tog, yo twice, SKP, k2—34 sts.

Row 12 Sl 1, k3, p1, p3tog, p1, k10, yo, SKP, k3, k2tog, yo, k8—32 sts.

Row 13 Sl 1, k8, yo, SKP, k1, k2tog, yo, k11, yo twice, SKP, k5—33 sts.

Row 14 Bind off 3 sts, k2, p1, k13, yo, SK2P, yo, k10—30 sts.

Rep rows 1 to 14 until desired length.

Bind off.

lilac leaf lace

▶ Cast on 30 sts.

Row 1 (RS) K3, yo, k2tog, k1, p2, k1, k2tog, k6, p2, yo, k1, yo, p2, k3, yo, k2tog, k1, yo twice, k2.

Row 2 K3, p1, k3, yo, k2tog, k3, p3, k2, p5, p2tog, p1, k5, yo, k2tog, k1.

Row 3 K3, yo, k2tog, k1, p2, k1, k2tog, k4, p2, [k1, yo] twice, k1, p2, k3, yo, k2tog, k5.

Row 4 K7, yo, k2tog, k3, p5, k2, p3, p2tog, p1, k5, yo, k2tog, k1.

Row 5 K3, yo, k2tog, k1, p2, k1, k2tog, k2, p2, k2, yo, k1, yo, k2, p2, k3, yo, k2tog, k1, [yo twice, k2tog] twice.

Row 6 [K2, p1] twice, k3, yo, k2tog, k3, p7, k2, p1, p2tog, p1, k5, yo, k2tog, k1.

Row 7 K3, yo, k2tog, k1, p2, k1, k2tog, p2, k3, yo, k1, yo, k3, p2, k3, yo, k2tog, k7.

Row 8 K9, yo, k2tog, k3, p9, k2, p2tog, k5, yo, k2tog, k1.

Row 9 K3, yo, k2tog, k1, p2, yo, k1, yo, p2, k1, k2tog, k6, p2, k3, yo, k2tog, k1, [yo twice, k2tog] 3 times.

Row 10 [K2, p1] 3 times, k3, yo, k2tog, k3, p5, p2tog, p1, k2, p3, k5, yo, k2tog, k1.

Row 11 K3, yo, k2tog, k1, p2, [k1, yo] twice, k1, p2, k1, k2tog, k4, p2, k3, yo, k2tog, k10.

Row 12 K12, yo, k2tog, k3, p3, p2tog, p1, k2, p5, k5, yo, k2tog, k1.

Row 13 K3, yo, k2tog, k1, p2, k2, yo, k1, yo, k2, p2, k1, k2tog, k2, p2, k3, yo, k2tog, k2, [yo twice, k2tog] 4 times.

Row 14 [K2, p1] 4 times, k4, yo, k2tog, k3, p1, p2tog, p1, k2, p7, k5, yo, k2tog, k1.

Row 15 K3, yo, k2tog, k1, p2, k3, yo, k1, yo, k3, p2, k1, k2tog, p2, k3, yo, k2tog, k14.

Row 16 Bind off 11 sts, k4, yo, k2tog, k3, p2tog, k2, p9, k5, yo, k2tog, k1.

Rep rows 1 to 16 until desired length, end with row 15.

Bind off.

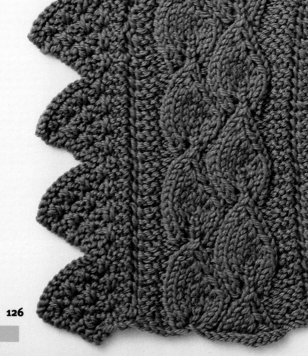

bountiful leaves

▶ Cast on 15 sts.

Row 1 (WS) Knit.

Row 2 K2, yo, p2tog, k2, yo twice, k2tog, yo, k1, yo, k2tog tbl, yo twice, k2, yo twice, k2—21 sts.

Row 3 K3, p1, k3, p7, k4, yo, p2tog, k1.

Row 4 K2, yo, p2tog, k2, yo twice, k2tog, k2, yo, k1, yo, k2, k2tog tbl, yo twice, k4, yo twice, k2—27 sts.

Row 5 K3, p1, k5, p11, k4, yo, p2tog, k1.

Row 6 K2, yo, p2tog, k2, yo twice, k2tog, k4, yo, k1, yo, k4, k2tog tbl, yo twice, k6, yo twice, k2—33 sts.

Row 7 K3, p1, k7, p15, k4, yo, p2tog, k1.

Row 8 K2, yo, p2tog, k3, yo twice, k3tog tbl, k9, k3tog, yo twice, k11.

Row 9 Bind off 8 sts, k3, p13, k5, yo, p2tog, k1—25 sts.

Row 10 K2, yo, p2tog, k4, yo twice, k3tog tbl, k7, k3tog, yo twice, k2, yo twice, k2—27sts.

Row 11 K3, p1, k3, p11, k6, yo, p2tog, k1.

Row 12 K2, yo, p2tog, k5, yo twice, k3tog tbl, k5, k3tog, yo twice, k5, yo twice, k2—29 sts.

Row 13 K3, p1, k6, p9, k7, yo, p2tog, k1.

Row 14 K2, yo, p2tog, k6, yo twice, k3tog tbl, k3, k3tog, yo twice, k8, yo twice, k2—31 sts.

Row 15 K3, p1, k9, p7, k8, yo, p2tog, k1.

Row 16 K2, yo, p2tog, k7, k3tog tbl, k4tog, pass the k3tog tbl over the k4tog (dec 6 sts), k13—25 sts.

Row 17 Bind off 10 sts, k2, p1, k8, yo, p2tog, k1—15 sts.

Rep rows 2 to 17 until desired length.

Bind off.

twining elm eyelet

▶ Cast on 17 sts.

Rows 1 and 3 (RS) K3, [yo, p2tog] twice, yo, k1 tbl, k2tog, p1, SKP, k1 tbl, yo, k3.

Rows 2 and 4 K3, p3, k1, p3, k2, [yo, p2tog] twice, k1.

Row 5 K3, [yo, p2tog] twice, yo, k1 tbl, yo, k2tog, p1, SKP, yo, k4—18 sts.

Row 6 K4, p2, k1, p4, k2, [yo, p2tog] twice, k1.

Row 7 K3, [yo, p2tog] twice, yo, k1 tbl, k1, k1 tbl, yo, S2KP, yo, k5—19 sts.

Row 8 K5, p7, k2, [yo, p2tog] twice, k1.

Row 9 K3, [yo, p2tog] twice, yo, k1 tbl, k3, k1 tbl, yo, k7—21 sts.

Row 10 Bind off 4 sts, k2, p7, k2, [yo, p2tog] twice, k1—17 sts.

Rep rows 1 to 10 until desired length.

Bind off.

nosegay pattern

▶ Cast on 16 sts.

Row 1 (WS) K7, p2, k7.

Row 2 P6, 2-st RC, 2-st LC, p6.

Row 3 K5, 1/1 LPC, p2, 1/1 RPC, k5.

Row 4 P4, 1/1 RPC, 2-st RC, 2-st LC, 1/1 LPC, p4.

Row 5 K3, 1/1 LPC, k1, p4, k1, 1/1 RPC, k3.

Row 6 P2, 1/1RPC, p1, 1/1 RPC, k2, 1/1LPC, p1, 1/1 LPC, p2.

Row 7 [K2, p1] twice, k1, p2, k1, [p1, k2] twice.

Row 8 P2, MB, p1, 1/1 RPC, p1, k2, p1, 1/1 LPC, p1, MB, p2.

Row 9 K4, p1, k2, p2, k2, p1, k4.

Row 10 P4, MB, p2, k2, p2, MB, p4.

Rep rows 1 to 10 until desired length.

Bind off.

twin leaf

▶ Cast on 22 sts.

Row 1 and all WS rows P10, k2, p10.

Row 2 K6, DD, yo, k1, yo, p2, yo, k1, yo, SK2P, k6.

Row 4 K4, DD, k1, [yo, k1] twice, p2, k1, [yo, k1] twice, SK2P, k4.

Row 6 K2, DD, k2, yo, k1, yo, k2, p2, k2, yo, k1, yo, k2, SK2P, k2.

Row 8 DD, k3, yo, k1, yo, k3, p2, k3, yo, k1, yo, k3, SK2P.

Rep rows 1 to 8 until desired length.

Bind off.

banana tree

▶ Cast on 18 sts.

Row 1 (RS) P3, 2-st RC, k1, 2-st RC, k2, p3, 1/1 LPC, k1, p2.

Row 2 K2, p2, k4, p2, k1, p3, 2-st RPC, k2.

Row 3 P2, k3, 1/1 RPC, p1, k1, 2-st LC, p3, 1/1 LPC, p2.

Row 4 K6, 2-st LPC, p2, k2, p4, k2.

Row 5 P2, k2, 1/1 RPC, p2, k1, 2-st LC twice, p5.

Row 6 K4, 2-st LPC, p4, k3, p3, k2.

Row 7 P2, k1, 1/1 RPC, p3, k2, 1/1 LPC, k1, 2-st LC, p3.

Row 8 K2, 2-st LPC, p3, k1, p2, k4, p2, k2.

Row 9 P2, 1/1 RPC, p3, 2-st RC, k1, p1, 1/1 LPC, k3, p2.

Row 10 K2, p4, k2, p2, 2-st RPC, k6.

Row 11 P5, 2-st RC twice, k1, p2, 1/1 LPC, k2, p2.

Row 12 K2, p3, k3, p4, 2-st RPC, k4.

Rep rows 1 to 12 until desired length.

Bind off.

128

flowing leaves

▶ Cast on 23 sts.

Row 1 (RS) Sl 1, k2, yo, k2tog, k1, yo, k1, yo, (sl 1, k3tog, pass the sl st over k3tog), yo, k1, yo, (k3tog and return to LH needle, pass 2nd st over k3tog and off needle, sl to RH needle), yo, k1, yo, k2, yo, k2tog, k2.

Row 2 and all WS rows Sl 1, k4, p13, k5.

Row 3 Sl 1, k2, yo, k2tog, k1, yo, k3, yo, SKP, k3tog and pass the second st on the RH needle over the it, yo, k3, yo, k2, yo, k2tog, k2.

Row 5 Sl 1, k2, yo, k2tog, k1, yo, SKP, k1, k2tog, yo, k1, yo, SKP, k1, k2tog, yo, k2, yo, k2tog, k2.

Row 7 Sl 1, k2, yo, k2tog, k1, yo, SKP, k1, k2tog, yo, k1, yo, SKP, k1, k2tog, yo, k2, yo, k2tog, k2.

Row 8 Rep row 2.

Rep rows 1 to 8 until desired length.

Bind off.

fancy leaf edging

▶ Cast on 13 sts.

Row 1 (RS) K1, SK2P, yo, k5, yo, k1 tbl, yo, SKP, k1.

Row 2 and all WS rows Purl.

Rows 3 and 5 K1, k1 tb1, yo, k1, k2tog tbl, p1, SKP, k1, yo, k1 tb1, yo, SKP, k1.

Row 7 K1, SKP, yo, k2tog tbl, p1, SKP, [yo, k1 tb1] twice, yo, SKP, k1.

Row 9 K1, SKP, yo, k3tog tbl, yo, k3, yo, k1 tb1, yo, SKP, k1.

Row 10 Rep row 2.

Rep rows 1 to 10 until desired length.

Bind off.

leaf vein insertion

▶ Cast on 18 sts.

Row 1 (RS) K3, k2tog, yo, k5, yo, k3, SKP, k3.

Row 2 and all WS rows K3, p12, k3.

Row 3 K3, k2tog, k5, yo, k1, yo, k2, SKP, k3.

Row 5 K3, k2tog, k4, yo, k3, yo, k1, SKP, k3.

Row 7 K3, k2tog, k3, yo, k5, yo, SKP, k3.

Row 9 K3, k2tog, k2, yo, k1, yo, k5, SKP, k3.

Row 11 K3, k2tog, k1, yo, k3, yo, k4, SKP, k3.

Row 12 Rep row 2.

Rep rows 1 to 12 until desired length.

Bind off.

quilted leaf pattern

▶ Cast on 9 sts.

Rows 1 and 3 (RS) Purl.

Rows 2 and 4 Knit.

Row 5 P2, p2tog, yo, k1 tbl, yo, p2tog, p2.

Row 6 K4, p1 tbl, k4.

Row 7 P1, p2tog, yo, k3 tbl, yo, p2tog, p1.

Row 8 K3, p3 tbl, k3.

Row 9 P2tog, yo, k5 tbl, yo, p2tog.

Row 10 K2, p5 tbl, k2.

Row 11 P1, yo, k2 tbl, SK2P, k2 tbl, yo, p1.

Row 12 Rep row 10.

Row 13 P2, yo, k1 tbl, SK2P, k1 tbl, yo, p2.

Row 14 Rep row 8.

Row 15 P3, yo, SK2P, yo, p3.

Row 16 Rep row 6.

Rep rows 1 to 16 until desired length.

Bind off.

leaf vein insertion with bobbles

Work as for **Leaf Vein Insertion** until desired length.
Make **Bobbles** (see page 164) separately and sewn in
place (see photo.)

floral bouquet

▲ (multiple of 11sts plus 2)

Make **Bobble (MB)**

[K1, p1] twice, k1 in next st—5 sts, turn, p5, turn, pass 2nd, 3rd, 4th and 5th sts over first st one at a time, then k tbl.

K 4 rows.

Rows 1 and 2 Knit.

Row 3 (RS) *K5, k2tog, yo, k4; rep from *, end k2.

Row 4 and all WS rows Purl.

Row 5 *K4, k2tog, yo, k1, yo, ssk, k2; rep from *, end k2.

Row 7 *K3, [k2tog, yo] twice, k1, yo, ssk, k1; rep from *, end k2.

Row 9 *K2, [k2tog, yo] twice, k1, [yo, ssk] twice; rep from *, end k2.

Row 11 *K3, k2tog, yo, k1, MB, k1, yo, ssk, k1; rep from *, end k2.

Row 13 *K4, MB, k3, MB, k2; rep from *, end k2.

Row 15 *K6, MB, k4; rep from *, end k2.

Row 16 Purl.

K 4 rows.

Cont as desired.

berry bunch

▲ (multiple of 16 sts plus 15)

Row 1 (WS) *P3, k1, p3, cast on 4 sts and p them, p4, k1, p3, k1; rep from *, end p3, k1, p3, cast on 4 sts and p them, p4, k1, p3.

Row 2 *K3, p1, k11, p1, k3, p1; rep from *, end k3, p1, k11, p1, k3.

Row 3 *P3, k1, p2, cast on 4 sts and p them, p1, p5tog, cast on 4 sts and p them, p3, k1, p3, k1; rep from *, end p3, k1, p2, cast on 4 sts and p them, p1, p5tog, cast on 4 sts and p them, p3, k1, p3.

Row 4 *K3, p1, k15, p1, k3, p1; rep from *, end k3, p1, k15, p1, k3.

Row 5 *P3, k1, p1, [cast on 4 sts and p them, p1, p5tog] twice, cast on 4 sts and p them, p2, k1, p3, k1; rep from *, end p3, k1, p1, [cast on 4 sts and p them, p1, p5tog] twice, cast on 4 sts and p them, p2, k1, p3.

Row 6 *K3, p1, k19, p1, k3, p1; rep from *, end k3, p1, k19, p1, k3.

Row 7 *P3, k1, [p1, p5tog] 3 times, p1, k1, p3, cast on 4 sts and p them, k1, rep from *, end p3, k1, [p1, p5tog] 3 times, p1, k1, p3.

Row 8 *[K3, p1] 3 times, k8, rep from *, end last rep k3.

Row 9 P3, *[k1, p3] twice, k1, p2, cast on 4 sts and p them, p1, p5tog, cast on 4 sts and p them, p3, rep from *, end [k1, p3] 3 times.

Row 10 K3, *[p1, k3] twice, p1, k15, rep from *, end [p1, k3] 3 times.

Row 11 P3, *[k1, p3] twice, k1, p1, [cast on 4 sts and p them, p1, p5tog] twice, cast on 4 sts and p them, p2, rep from *, end [k1, p3] 3 times.

Row 12 K3, *[p1, k3] twice, p1, k19; rep from *, end [p1, k3] 3 times.

Row 13 P3, *k1, p3, cast on 4 sts and p them, k1, p3, k1, [p1, p5tog] 3 times, p1; rep from *, end k1, p3, cast on 4 sts and p them, k1, p3, k1, p3.

Row 14 K3, *p1, k11, p1, k7; rep from *, end p1, k11, p1, k3.

Cont as desired.

blooming flower

▲ (multiple of 17 sts plus 2)

Rows 1 and 2 Knit.

Row 3 (WS) K2, *k6, p1, k1, p1, k8; rep from * to end.

Row 4 *P8, k1, p1, k1, p6; rep from *, end p2.

Row 5 K2, *k5, p2, k1, p2, k7; rep from * to end.

Row 6 *P7, k2, p1, k2, p5; rep from *, end p2.

Row 7 K2, *k4, p3, k1, p3, k6; rep from * to end.

Row 8 *P6, k3, p1, k3, p4; rep from *, end p2.

Row 9 K2, *k3, p4, k1, p4, k5; rep from * to end.

Row 10 *P5, k1, k2tog, k1, yo, k1, yo, k1, ssk, k1, p3; rep from *, end p2.

Row 11 K2, *k2, p4, k1, p1, k1, p4, k4; rep from * to end.

Row 12 *P4, k1, k2tog, k1, yo, p1, k1, p1, yo, k1, ssk, k1, p2; rep from *, end p2.

Row 13 K2, *k1, p4, k2, p1, k2, p4, k3; rep from * to end.

Row 14 *P3, k1, k2tog, k1, yo, p2, k1, p2, yo, k1, ssk, k1, p1; rep from *, end p2.

Row 15 K2, *p4, k3, p1, k3, p4, k2; rep from * to end.

Row 16 *P2, k1, k2tog, k1, yo, p3, k1, p3, yo, k1, ssk, k1; rep from *, end p2.

Row 17 K2, *p3, k4, p1, k4, p3, k2; rep from * to end.

Row 18 *P2, k2tog, k1, yo, p3, MB, p1, MB, p3, yo, k1, ssk; rep from *, end p2.

Row 19 K2, *p1, k13, p1, k2; rep from * to end.

Row 20 *P6, MB, p5, MB, p4; rep from *, end p2.

Rows 21, 23, 25, 27 and 29 Knit.

Row 22 *P5, MB, p1, [p2tog, yo] twice, p2, MB, p3; rep from *, end p2.

Row 24 *P5, MB, [p2tog, yo] 3 times, p1, MB, p3; rep from *, end p2.

Row 26 Rep row 22.

Row 28 *P6, MB, p5, MB, p4; rep from *, end p2.

Row 30 *P8, MB, p1, MB, p6; rep from *, end p2.

Row 31 Knit.

Cont as desired.

berry cluster I

▲ (multiple of 23 sts)

K 2 rows.

Row 1 (RS) *K8, k2tog, yo, k1, p1, k1, yo, ssk, k8; rep from * to end.

Row 2 *P7, p2tog tbl, p2, yo, k1, yo, p2, p2tog, p7; rep from * to end.

Row 3 *K6, k2tog, k1, yo, k2, p1, k2, yo, k1, ssk, k6; rep from * to end.

Row 4 *P5, p2tog tbl, p3, yo, p1, k1, p1, yo, p3, p2tog, p5; rep from * to end.

Row 5 *K4, k2tog, k2, yo, k3, p1, k3, yo, k2, ssk, k4; rep from * to end.

Row 6 *P3, p2tog tbl, p4, yo, p2, k1, p2, yo, p4, p2tog, p3; rep from * to end.

Row 7 *K2, k2tog, k3, yo, k4, p1, k4, yo, k3, ssk, k2; rep from * to end.

Row 8 *P1, p2tog tbl, p5, yo, p3, k1, p3, yo, p5, p2tog, p1; rep from * to end.

Row 9 *K2tog, k4, yo, k5, p1, k5, yo, k4, ssk; rep from * to end.

Row 10 *P11, k1, p11; rep from * to end.

Row 11 *K11, p1, k11; rep from * to end.

Row 12 Rep row 10.

K 4 rows.

Cont as desired.

Make **Bobbles** (see page 164) and sew to clusters at lower edge.

berry cluster II with beads

Work rows 1 to 12 of Berry Cluster twice.

K 4 rows.

Cont as desired.

Sew beads to clusters (see photo).

kings bounty

▲ (multiple of 13 sts)

Rows 1 and 2 Knit.

Row 3 (RS) *P6, MB, p6; rep from * to end.

Rows 4 and 6 Knit.

Row 5 Purl.

Row 7 *P4, MB, p3, MB, p4; rep from * to end.

Row 8 *K4, p5, k4; rep from * to end.

Row 9 *P3, k2tog, [k1, yo] twice, k1, SKP, p3; rep from * to end.

Row 10 *K3, p7, k3; rep from *, to end.

Row 11 *P2, k2tog, k2, yo, k1, yo, k2, SKP, p2; rep from * to end.

Row 12 *K2, p9, k2; rep from * to end.

Row 13 *P1, k2tog, k3, yo, k1, yo, k3, SKP, p1; rep from * to end.

Row 14 *K1, p11, k1; rep from * to end.

Row 15 *P1, k1, k2tog, yo, SKP, yo, k1, yo, k2tog, yo, SKP, k1, p1; rep from * to end.

Row 16 *K1, p2, k1, p5, k1, p2, k1; rep from * to end.

Row 17 *P1, k2tog, yo, p1, yo, SKP, k1, k2tog, yo, p1, yo, SKP, p1; rep from * to end.

Row 18 *K1, p1, k3, p3, k3, p1, k1; rep from * to end.

Row 19 *P5, yo, SK2P, yo, p5; rep from * to end.

Row 20 *K6, p1, k6; rep from * to end.

Rows 21 and 22 Knit.

Cont as desired.

133

floral lace and cables

- Cable pat may be worked at beg and end of multiple reps of lace pat or between each rep of lace pat.

▲ **Cable Pattern** (over 8 sts)

Rows 1 and 3 P2, k4, p2.

Rows 2 and 4 K2, p4, k2.

Row 5 P2, 4-st RC, p2.

Row 6 Rep row 2.

Rep rows 1 to 6 for cable pat.

Lace Pattern (multiple of 18 sts plus 1)

Row 1 (RS) K1, *yo, SKP, p3, yo, SKP, k3, k2tog, yo, p3, k2tog, yo, k1; rep from * to end.

Row 2 and all WS rows K the knit sts, p the purl sts and p the yo sts.

Row 3 K1, *yo, k1, SKP, p3, yo, SKP, k1, k2tog, yo, p3, k2tog, k1, yo, k1; rep from * to end.

Row 5 K1, *yo, k2, SKP, p3, yo, SK2P, yo, p3, k2tog, k2, yo, k1; rep from * to end.

Row 7 K1, *yo, k3, SKP, p7, k2tog, k3, yo, k1; rep from * to end.

Row 9 K1, *yo, k4, SKP, p5, k2tog, k4, yo, k1; rep from * to end.

Row 11 K1, *yo, k5, SKP, p3, k2tog, k5, yo, k1; rep from * to end.

Row 13 K1, *yo, k6, SKP, p1, k2tog, k6, yo, k1; rep from * to end.

Row 15 K1, *yo, k2, k2tog, yo, SKP, k2, p1, k2, k2tog, yo, SKP, k2, yo, k1; rep from * to end.

Row 17 K1, *k2, k2tog, yo, p1, yo, SKP, k1, p1, k1, k2tog, yo, p1, yo, SKP, k3; rep from * to end.

Row 19 K1, *k1, k2tog, yo, p3, yo, SKP, p1, k2tog, yo, p3, yo, SKP, k2; rep from * to end.

Row 21 K1, *k2tog, yo, p3, k2tog, [k1, yo] twice, k1, SKP, p3, yo, SKP, k1; rep from * to end.

Row 23 K2tog, *yo, p3, k2tog, k2, yo, k1, yo, k2, SKP, p3, yo, SK2P; rep from *, end last rep SKP.

Row 25 P1, *p3, k2tog, k3, yo, k1, yo, k3, SKP, p4; rep from * to end.

Row 27 P1, *p2, k2tog, k4, yo, k1, yo, k4, SKP, p3; rep from * to end.

Row 29 P1, *p1, k2tog, k5, yo, k1, yo, k5, SKP, p2; rep from * to end.

Row 31 P1, *k2tog, k6, yo, k1, yo, k6, SKP, p1; rep from * to end.

Row 33 P1, *k2, k2tog, yo, SKP, k2, yo, k1, yo, k2, k2tog, yo, SKP, k2, p1; rep from * to end.

Row 35 P1, *k1, k2tog, yo, p1, yo, SKP, k5, k2tog, yo, p1, yo, SKP, k1, p1; rep from * to end.

Row 36 Rep row 2.

Rep rows 1 to 36 for lace pat.

Cont as desired.

flowers of lace

 (multiple of 21 sts)

K 4 rows.

Row 1 (WS) Purl.

Row 2 *K8, k2tog, yo, k1, yo, ssk, k8; rep from * to end.

Row 3 *P7, p2tog tbl, yo, p3, yo, p2tog, p7; rep from * to end.

Row 4 *K6, k2tog, yo, k1, yo, SK2P, yo, k1, yo, ssk, k6; rep from * to end.

Row 5 *P5, k2tog tbl, yo, p7, yo, p2tog, p5; rep from * to end.

Row 6 *K4, k2tog, yo, k3, yo, SK2P, yo, k3, yo, ssk, k4; rep from * to end.

Row 7 *P3, k2tog tbl, yo, p11, yo, p2tog, p3; rep from * to end.

Row 8 *K2, k2tog, yo, k5, yo, SK2P, yo, k5, yo, ssk, k2; rep from * to end.

Rows 9 to 15 Rep rows 1 to 7.

Row 16 *K1, k2tog, yo, k1, yo, ssk, k3, yo, SK2P, yo, k3, k2tog, yo, k1, yo, ssk, k1; rep from * to end.

Rows 17, 19, 21, 23, 25 and 27 Purl.

Row 18 *K2tog, yo, k3, yo, ssk, k2, yo, SK2P, yo, k2, k2tog, yo, k3, yo, ssk; rep from * to end.

Row 20 *K2, yo, SK2P, yo, k3, k2tog, yo, k1, yo, ssk, k3, yo, SK2P, yo, k2; rep from * to end.

Row 22 *K7, k2tog, yo, k3, yo, ssk, k7; rep from * to end.

Row 24 *K9, yo, SK2P, yo, k9; rep from * to end.

Row 26 Knit.

Row 28 Purl.

K 4 rows.

Cont as desired.

drooping elm

 (multiple of 15 sts plus 1)

Row 1 (RS) *K1, yo, k1, ssk, p1, k2tog, k1, yo, p1, ssk, p1, k2tog, yo, k1, yo; rep from *, end k1.

Row 2 P1, *p4, k1, p1, k1, p3, k1, p4; rep from * to end.

Row 3 *K1, yo, k1, ssk, p1, k2tog, k1, p1, SK2P, yo, k3, yo; rep from *, end k1.

Row 4 P1, *p6, k1, p2, k1, p4; rep from * to end.

Row 5 *[K1, yo] twice, ssk, p1, k2tog twice, yo, k5, yo; rep from *, end k1.

Row 6 P1, *p7, k1, p1, k1, p5; rep from * to end.

Row 7 *K1, yo, k3, yo, SK2P, p1, yo, k1, ssk, p1, k2tog, k1, yo; rep from *, end k1.

Row 8 P1, *[p3, k1] twice, p7; rep from * to end.

Row 9 *K1, yo, k5, yo, ssk, k1, ssk, p1, k2tog, k1, yo; rep from *, end k1.

Row 10 P1, *p3, k1, p2, k1, p8; rep from * to end.

Rows 11 to 14 Rep rows 1 to 4.

Cont as desired.

flora

cloisters

▲ (multiple of 10 sts plus 3)

MB

[K1, p1] twice, k1 in next st—5 sts, pass the 2nd, 3rd, 4th and 5th sts over first st.

Rows 1, 3 and 5 K3, *p7, k3; rep from * to end.

Rows 2, 4 and 6 P3, *k7, p3; rep from * to end.

Row 7 K2, *yo, ssk, p5, k2tog, yo, k1; rep from *, end k1.

Row 8 P4 *k5, p5; rep from *, end last rep p4.

Row 9 K3, *yo, ssk, p3, k2tog, yo, k3; rep from * to end.

Row 10 P5 *k3, p7; rep from *, end last rep p5.

Row 11 K2, *[yo, ssk] twice, p1, [k2tog, yo] twice, k1; rep from *, end k1.

Row 12 P6, *k1, p9; rep from *, end last rep p6.

Row 13 K3, *yo, ssk, yo, SK2P, yo, k2tog, yo, k3; rep from * to end.

Rows 14, 16 and 18 Purl.

Row 15 K4, *yo, ssk, k1, k2tog, yo, k5; rep from *, end last rep k4.

Row 17 K5, *yo, SK2P, yo, k7; rep from *, end last rep k5.

Row 19 K3, *p3, MB, p3, k3; rep from * to end.

Row 20 P3, *k7, p3; rep from * to end.

Work in k3, p7 rib or cont as desired.

spruce

▼ (multiple of 15 sts)

Row 1 (RS) *K7, yo, SKP, k6; rep from * to end.

Rows 2, 4, 6, 8 and 10 Purl.

Row 3 *K5, k2tog, yo, k1, yo, SKP, k5; rep from * to end.

Row 5 *K4, k2tog, yo, k3, yo, SKP, k4; rep from * to end.

Row 7 *K4, yo, SKP, yo, SK2P, yo, k2tog, yo, k4; rep from * to end.

Row 9 *K2, k2tog, yo, k1, yo, SKP, k1, k2tog, yo, k1, yo, SKP, k2; rep from * to end.

Row 11 *K2, [yo, SKP] twice, k3, [k2tog, yo] twice, k2; rep from * to end.

Row 12 *P3, [yo, p2tog] twice, p1, [p2tog tbl, yo] twice, p3; rep from * to end.

Row 13 *K4, yo, SKP, yo, SK2P, yo, k2tog, yo, k4; rep from * to end.

Row 14 *P5, yo, p2tog, p1, p2tog tbl, yo, p5; rep from * to end.

Row 15 *K6, yo, SK2P, yo, k6; rep from * to end.

Row 16 Purl.

Row 17 K3, p2, k4, p2, *k7, p2, k4, p2; rep from *, end k4.

Rows 18, 20 and 22 P4, k2, p4, k2,*p7, k2, p4, k2; rep from *, end p3.

Row 19 K3, p2, 4-st LC, p2, *k7, p2, 4-st LC, p2; rep from *, end k4.

Row 21 Rep row 17.

Row 23 Rep row 19.

Bind off knitwise.

traveling leaf pattern

▲ (multiple of 10 sts plus 1)

Row 1 *K1 A, p3 A, yo B, p2 B, p4 A; rep from *, end k1 A.

Row 2 *K5 A, k1 B, sl next st, drop yo, k3 A; rep from *, end k1 A.

Row 3 *K1 A, p3 A, sl 1, p1 B, yo, p1 B, p3 A; rep from *, end k1 A.

Row 4 *K4 A, sl 1 B, drop yo, k1 B, drop next st and leave to front, k2 A, pick up drop st and k in A, k1 A; rep from *, end k1 A.

Row 5 *K1 A, p3 A, yo B, p2 B, sl 1 B, p3 A; rep from *, end k1 A,

Row 6 *K2 A, sl 2 B, drop next st and leave to front, sl 2 back to LH needle, k drop st A, k2 B, k1 B, sl 1, drop yo, k3 A; rep from *, end k1 A.

Rep rows 3 to 6 until desired length.

Cont as desired.

bramble bush

▲ (multiple of 10 sts plus 11)

Row 1 (RS) Purl.

Row 2 Knit.

Row 3 P3, *p2tog, (k1, p1, k1) in next st (inc 2), p2tog, p5; rep from *, end last rep p3.

Row 4 K4, p3, k1, *k6, p3, k1; rep from *, end k3.

Row 5 P3, *RT, k1, LT, p5; rep from *, end last rep p3.

Row 6 K3, (p1, k1) twice, p1, *k5, (p1, k1) twice, p1; rep from * end k3.

Row 7 P3, *MB, p1, k1, p1, MB, p5; rep from *, end last rep p3.

Row 8 K3, k1 tbl, k1, p1, k1, k1 tbl, *k5, k1 tbl, k1, p1, k1, k1 tbl; rep from *, end k3.

Row 9 P3, *p2, MB, p7; rep from *, end last rep p5.

Row 10 K5, k1 tbl, k2, *k7, k1 tbl, k2; rep from *, end k3.

Row 11 Purl.

Row 12 Knit.

Row 13 P3, *p5, p2tog, inc 2, p2tog; rep from *, end p8.

Row 14 K8, *k1, p3, k6; rep from *, end last rep k9.

Row 15 P3, *p5, RT, k1, LT; rep from *, end p8.

Row 16 K8, *(p1, k1) twice, p1, k5; rep from *, end last rep k8.

Row 17 P3, *p5, MB, p1, k1, p1, MB; rep from *, end last rep p8.

Row 18 K8, *k1tbl, k1, p1, k1, k1tbl, k5; rep from *, end k3.

Row 19 P3, *p7, MB, p2; rep from *, end p8.

Row 20 K8, *k2, k1tbl, k7; rep from *, end k3.

Continue as desired.

cob nut stitch

▲ (multiple of 4 sts)

Row 1 (RS) *P3, [k1, yo, k1] in next st; rep from * to end.

Rows 2 and 3 *P3, k3; rep from * to end.

Row 4 *P3tog, k3; rep from * to end.

Row 5 Purl.

Row 6 Knit.

Row 7 *P1, [k1, yo, k1] in next st, p2; rep from * to end.

Row 8 K2, *p3, k3; rep from *, end p3, k1.

Row 9 P1, k3, *p3, k3; rep from *, end p2.

Row 10 K2, *p3tog, k3; rep from *, end p3tog, k1.

Row 11 Purl.

Row 12 Knit.

Rep rows 1 to 12 once.

Cont as desired.

palm tree puff

▲ (multiple of 10 sts plus 4)

Row 1 (RS) P4, *k1, p4, yo, k1, yo, p4; rep from * to end.

Row 2 K4, *yo, p3, yo, k4, p1, k4; rep from * to end.

Row 3 P4, *k1, p4, yo, k5, yo, p4; rep from * to end.

Row 4 K4, *yo, p7, yo, k4, p1, k4; rep from * to end.

Row 5 P4, *k1, p4, yo, k9, yo, p4; rep from * to end.

Row 6 K4, *p2tog, p7, p2tog tbl, k4, p1, k4; rep from * to end.

Row 7 P4, *k1, p4, ssk, k5, k2tog, p4; rep from * to end.

Row 8 K4, *p2tog, p3, p2tog tbl, k4, p1, k4; rep from * to end.

Row 9 P4, *k1, p4, ssk, k1, k2tog, p4; rep from * to end.

Row 10 K4, *p3tog, k4, p1, k4; rep from * to end.

Row 11 P4, *yo, k1, yo, p4, k1, p4; rep from * to end.

Row 12 K4, *p1, k4, yo, p3, yo, k4; rep from * to end.

Row 13 P4, *yo, k5, yo, p4, k1, p4; rep from * to end.

Row 14 K4, *p1, k4, yo, p7, yo, k4; rep from * to end.

Row 15 P4, *yo, k9, yo, p4, k1, p4; rep from * to end.

Row 16 K4, *p1, k4, p2tog, p7, p2tog tbl, k4; rep from * to end.

Row 17 P4, *ssk, k5, k2tog, p4, k1, p4; rep from * to end.

Row 18 K4, *p1, k4, p2tog, p3, p2tog tbl, k4; rep from * to end.

Row 19 P4, *ssk, k1, k2tog, p4, k1, p4; rep from * to end.

Row 20 K4, *p1, k4, p3tog, k4; rep from * to end.

Rep rows 1 to 10 once more.

Cont as desired.

embossed snowflake

▲ (multiple of 43 sts plus 30)

Knit 4 rows.

Row 1 (WS) Purl.

Rows 2 and 22 K3, *k8, p1, k9, p1, k24; rep from *, end k5, p1, k9, p1, k11.

Rows 3 and 21 P11, k2, p7, k2, p5, *p24, k2, p7, k2, p8; rep from *, end p3.

Row 4 and 20 K3, *k8, p3, k5, p3, k24; rep from * to last 27 sts, end k5, p3, k5, p3, k11.

Rows 5 and 19 P11, k4, p3, k4, p5, *p24, k4, p3, k4, p8; rep from *, end p3.

Rows 6 and 18 K3, *k8, p5, k1, p5, k14, p1, k9; rep from * to last 27 sts, end k5, p5, k1, p5, k11.

Rows 7 and 17 P6, k5, p1, k4, p1, k4, p1, k5, *p8, k3, p8, k5, p1, k4, p1, k4, p1, k5, p3; rep from *, end p3.

Rows 8 and 16 K3, *k4, p5, (k1, p3) twice, k1, p5, k8, p2, k1, p2, k7; rep from * to last 27 sts, end k1, p5, (k1, p3) twice, k1, p5, k7.

Rows 9 and 15 P8, k5, (p1, k2) twice, p1, k5, p2, *p6, k2, p1, k1, p1, k2, p8, k5, (p1, k2) twice, p1, k5, p5; rep from *, end p3.

Rows 10 and 14 K3, *k6, p5, (k1, p1) twice, k1, p5, k8, p2, (k1, p1) twice, k1, p2, k5; rep from * to last 27 sts, end k3, p5, (k1, p1) twice, k1, p5, k9.

Rows 11 and 13 P10, k5, p3, k5, p4, *p4, k2, (p1, k1) 3 times, p1, k2, p8, k5, p3, k5, p7; rep from *, end p3.

Row 12 K3, *k8, p5, k1, p5, k8, p2, (k1, p1) 4 times, k1, p2, k3; rep from * to last 27 sts, end k5, p5, k1, p5, k11.

Row 23 Purl.

Knit 4 rows.

Cont as desired.

hearts

▲ (multiple of 15 sts)

Rows 1 and 3 (RS) Purl.

Row 2 Knit.

Row 4 *K7, [p1 tbl, p1, p1 tbl] in next st, k7; rep from * to end.

Row 5 *P7, k3, p7; rep from * to end.

Row 6 *K5, k2tog, p1, [p1 tbl, p1, p1 tbl] in next st, p1, k2tog, k5; rep from * to end.

Row 7 *P6, k5, p6; rep from * to end.

Row 8 *K4, k2tog, p2, [p1 tbl, p1, p1 tbl] in next st, p2, k2tog, k4; rep from * to end.

Row 9 *P5, k7, p5; rep from * to end.

Row 10 *K3, k2tog, p3, [p1 tbl, p1, p1 tbl] in next st, p3, k2tog, k3; rep from * to end.

Row 11 *P4, k9, p4; rep from * to end.

Row 12 *K4, p4, [p1 tbl, p1, p1 tbl] in next st, p4, k4; rep from * to end.

Row 13 *P4, k5, p1, k5, p4; rep from * to end.

Row 14 *K4, p5, [k1, yo, k1] in next st, p5, k4; rep from * to end.

Row 15 *P4, k5, p3, k5, p4; rep from * to end.

Row 16 *K4, dec 5, inc 1, k1, inc 1, dec 5, k4; rep from * to end.

Cont as desired.

embossed hearts

▲ (multiple of 12 sts plus 9)

K 2 rows.

Row 1 (RS) P4, k1, *p11, k1; rep from *, end p4.

Row 2 K3, p3, *k9, p3; rep from *, end k3.

Row 3 P3, k3, *p9, k3; rep from *, end p3.

Row 4 K2, p5, *k7, p5; rep from *, end k2.

Row 5 P1, k7, *p5, k7; rep from *, end p1.

Row 6 P9, *k3, p9; rep from * to end.

Row 7 K9, *p3, k9; rep from * to end.

Row 8 Rep row 6.

Row 9 K4, p1, *k4, p3, k4, p1; rep from *, end k4.

Row 10 K1, p2, k3, p2, *k5, p2, k3, p2; rep from *, end k1.

Row 11 Purl.

Rows 12 and 13 Knit.

Row 14 Purl.

Cont as desired.

butterfly

▲ (multiple of 18 sts plus 1)

Rows 1 and 3 (RS) Knit.

Rows 2 and 4 Purl.

Rows 5 and 13 *K3, p4, k5, p4, k2; rep from *, end last rep k3.

Rows 6 and 12 *P4, k4, p3, k4, p3; rep from *, end last rep p4.

Rows 7 and 11 *K5, p4, k1, p4, k4; rep from *, end last rep k5.

Rows 8 and 10 *P6, k3, p1, k3, p5; rep from *, end last rep p6.

Row 9 Knit.

Rows 14, 16 and 18 Purl.

Rows 15 and 17 Knit.

Cont as desired.

Embroider 2 antennae on each butterfly (see photo).

points

picots

horizontal garter band

▲ (over any number of sts)

Row 1 Knit.

Rep row 1 until desired length.

Cont as desired.

garter stitch color blocks

▲ (multiple of 7 sts)

With A, cast on a multiple of 7 sts per color used.

Row 1 (RS) *K7 B, K7 C, K7 D; rep from * to end.

Work in garter st for 11 rows (6 ridges), working colors as established. Change to A.

Cont as desired.

bobble stitch garter edging

▲ (multiple of 6 sts plus 5)

Row 1 (WS) Knit.

Row 2 K2, *MB, k5; rep from *, end last rep MB, k2.

Work even in garter st until desired length.

Cont as desired.

vertical garter band

▶ (over any number of sts)

Determine width of the edging, then knit a swatch in garter st to determine number of sts needed.

Work in garter st until desired length. Bind off.

With RS facing, pick up and k evenly along one side edge of band. Beg with a WS row and cont as desired.

picots

garter slip stitch

▲ (multiple of 2 sts plus 1)

• Sl all sts purlwise.

Rows 1 and 2 Knit.

Row 3 (RS) K1, *sl 1, k1; rep from * to end.

Row 4 K1, *sl 1 wyif, k1 wyib; rep from * to end.

Rows 5 and 6 Knit.

Row 7 K2, *sl 1, k1; rep from *, end k2.

Row 8 K2, *sl 1 wyif, k1 wyib; rep from *, end k2.

Rep rows 1 to 8 until desired length.

Cont as desired.

3-color garter slip stitch

▲ (multiple of 2 sts plus 1)

Work as for garter slip stitch as foll:

*2 rows A, 2 rows B, 2 rows C; rep from * until desired length.

Cont as desired.

2-color garter slip stitch

▲ (multiple of 2 sts plus 1)

Work rows 1 to 8 of Garter Slip Stitch as foll:

*2 rows A, 2 rows B; rep from * until desired length.

Cont as desired.

garter line stitch

▲ (multiple of 6 sts plus 1)

Row 1 (RS) P1, *k5, p1; rep from * to end.

Row 2 Purl.

Rep rows 1 and 2 until desired length.

Cont as desired.

garter ridge with rolled edge

▲ (over any number of sts)

Work in St st for 1"/2.5cm.

Row 1 and 3 (RS) Knit.

Row 2 Purl.

Row 4 Knit.

Rep rows 1 to 4 until desired length.

Cont as desired.

garter shutter

▲ (multiple of 5 sts plus 2)

Row 1 (RS) K2, *p3, k2; rep from * to end.

Row 2 Purl.

Rep rows 1 and 2 until desired length.

Cont as desired.

stacked garter stitch

▲ (multiple of 9 sts plus 2)

Row 1 (RS) K2, *p2, k3, p2, k2; rep from * to end.

Rows 2 and 4 Purl.

Row 3 K2, *p7, k2; rep from * to end.

Rep rows 1 to 4 until desired length.

Cont as desired.

garter brick stitch

▲ (multiple of 12 sts plus 8)

Row 1 (RS) P8, *k4, p8; rep from * to end.

Row 2 K8, *p4, k8; rep from * to end.

Row 3 P2, *k4, p8; rep from *, end last rep p2.

Row 4 K2, *p4, k8; rep from *, end last rep k2.

Rep rows 1 to 4 until desired length.

Cont as desired.

picots

caterpillar

▲ (multiple of 10 sts plus 6)

Row 1 (RS) P6, *k4, p6; rep from * to end.

Rows 2 and 4 Purl.

Row 3 P1, *k4, p6; rep from *, end last rep p1.

Rep rows 1 to 4 until desired length.

Cont as desired.

garter stitch weave

▲ (multiple of 11 sts)

Row 1 (RS) *P3, [k1, p3] twice; rep from * to end.

Row 2 *K3, [p1, k3] twice; rep from * to end.

Row 3 Knit.

Row 4 *K5, p1, k5; rep from * to end.

Row 5 *P5, k1, p5; rep from * to end.

Row 6 Purl.

Rep rows 1 to 6 until desired length.

Cont as desired.

garter box stitch

▲ (multiple of 4 sts plus 1)

Row 1 (RS) Knit.

Rows 2 and 4 Purl.

Row 3 K1, *p3, k1; rep from * to end.

Rep rows 1 to 4 until desired length.

Cont as desired.

block garter

▲ (multiple of 4 sts plus 2)

Row 1 (RS) Purl.

Row 2 Knit.

Row 3 K2, *p2, k2; rep from * to end.

Row 4 P2, *k2, p2; rep from * to end.

Rep rows 1 to 4 until desired length.

Cont as desired.

diagonal garter stitch

▲ (multiple of 5 sts plus 2)

Row 1 and all RS rows Knit.

Row 2 P2, *k3, p2; rep from * to end.

Row 4 K1, *p2, k3; rep from *, p1.

Row 6 K2, *p2, k3; rep from * to end.

Row 8 *K3, p2; rep from *, end last rep, k2.

Row 10 P1, *k3, p2; rep from *, end k1.

Rep rows 1 to 10 until desired length.

Cont as desired.

the almonds

▲ (multiple of 4 sts plus 1)

Row 1 and all WS rows Purl.

Row 2 (RS) Purl.

Row 4 P2, *[k1, p1, k1] in next st, p3; rep from *, end last rep, p2.

Rows 6 and 8 P2, *k3, p3; rep from *, end last rep, p2.

Row 10 P2, *k3tog tbl, p3; rep from *, end last rep, p2.

Rows 12 and 13 Purl.

Rep rows 2 to 13 once more (or for desired length), then rows 2 and 3 once more.

Cont as desired.

picots

double welted edge

▲ (over any number of sts)

With A, work in St st for 11 rows.

Next row (WS) *Lift horizontal thread from cast-on edge below st on needle and place on LH needle, then p this thread tog with st on needle; rep from * for each st.

Work 11 rows more in St st.

Change to B and work in St st for 11 rows.

Next row (WS) *Lift horizontal thread from 11 rows below st on needle and place on LH needle, then p this thread tog with st on needle; rep from * for each st.

Cont in St st or as desired.

picot hem

▲ and ▼ (multiple of 2 sts plus 1)

• This edging can be used on a cast-on or bound-off edge.

Rows 1 and 3 (RS) Knit.

Row 2 and all WS rows Purl.

Row 5 (picot row) K1 *yo, k2tog; rep from * to end.

Row 6 Rep row 2.

Cont as desired.

Fold lower edge to WS at picot row and sew in place.

picot wave

▲ (multiple of 8 sts plus 2)

Work in St st for ½"/1.5cm, end with a WS row.

Next (picot) row (RS) *K2, yo, k2tog; rep from *, end k2.

Beg with a WS row and cont in St st for ¾"/2cm more, end with a WS row.

Next (cable) row (RS) K2, *sl next 2 sts to cn and hold to back, k2, k2 from cn, k4; rep from * to end.

Beg with a WS row and cont in St st or as desired.

Fold lower edge to WS at picot edge and sew in place.

folded hem

▲ (over any number of sts)

Work in St st for 1"/2.5cm, end with a RS row.

K next row on WS for turning ridge.

Cont in St st or as desired.

Fold lower edge to WS at turning ridge and sew in place.

147

picot point chain edging

▼ (over even number of sts)

• This edging is worked on the last row of a piece.

Last row (RS) Bind off 2 sts, *sl st back to LH needle, using the cable cast-on method, cast on 3 sts, then bind off 5 sts; rep from * to end. Fasten off.

chain edging

▲ (beg as multiple of 29 sts and end as multiple of 8 sts)

• Cast using the Knitting-on method.

Row 1 *K3 tbl, [M1, drop 3 sts off LH needle, k2tog tbl] 4 times, M1, drop 3 sts off LH needle, k3; rep from * to end.

Rows 2 and 4 Purl.

Row 3 *K2 tbl, SKP twice, SK2P, k2tog twice, k2; rep from * to end.

K 4 rows.

Cont as desired.

double bear paws

▲ (multiple of 16 sts plus 1)

Row 1 (RS) K1, *yo, [k1, p1] 7 times, k1, yo, k1; rep from * to end.

Row 2 K1, *p2, [k1, p1] 7 times, p1, k1; rep from * to end.

Row 3 K2, *yo, [k1, p1] 7 times, k1, yo, k3; rep from *, end last rep k2.

Row 4 K2, *p2, [k1, p1] 7 times, p1, k3; rep from *, end last rep k2.

Row 5 K3, *yo, [k1, p1] 7 times, k1, yo, k5; rep from *, end last rep k3.

Row 6 K3, *p2, [k1, p1] 7 times, p1, k5; rep from *, end last rep k3.

Row 7 K4, *yo, [k1, p1] 7 times, k1, yo, k7; rep from *, end last rep k4.

Row 8 K4, *p2, [k1, p1] 7 times, p1, k7; rep from *, end last rep k4.

Row 9 K5, *ssk 3 times, SK2P, k2tog 3 times, k9; rep from *, end last rep k5.

Row 10 Purl.

Cont as desired.

picot chain loops

▶ (Multiple of 5 sts)

Row 1 Knit.

Row 2 Bind off 2 sts, *sl st back to LH needle, [using cable cast-on method, cast on 2 sts, bind off next 2 sts, sl st back to LH needle] 3 times, using cable cast-on method, cast on 2 sts, bind off 6 sts; rep from * to end. Fasten off.

picots

bear tracks

▲ (multiple of 23 sts)

Row 1 (RS) *K2, [p4, k1] 3 times, p4, k2; rep from * to end.

Row 2 and all WS rows K the knit sts and p the purl sts.

Row 3 *K1, yo, k1, p2, p2tog, [k1, p4] twice, k1, p2tog, p2, k1, yo, k1; rep from * to end.

Row 5 *K2, yo, k1, p3, k1, p2, p2tog, k1, p2tog, p2, k1, p3, k1, yo, k2; rep from * to end.

Row 7 *K3, yo, k1, p1, p2tog, [k1, p3] twice, k1, p2tog, p1, k1, yo, k3; rep from * to end.

Row 9 *K4, yo, k1, p2, k1, p1, p2tog, k1, p2tog, p1, k1, p2, k1, yo, k4; rep from * to end.

Row 11 *K5, yo, k1, p2tog, [k1, p2] twice, k1, p2tog, k1, yo , k5; rep from * to end.

Row 13 *K6, yo, k1, p1, k1, [p2tog, k1] twice, p1, k1, yo, k6; rep from * to end.

Row 14 Rep row 2.

Work 2 rows in rev St st.

Cont as desired.

brunhilda's broom border

▲ (multiple of 21 sts plus 3)

Row 1 (RS) K1, *yo, k21; rep from *, end last rep k23.

Row 2 P2, *[p1, k3] 5 times, p2; rep from *, end last rep p3.

Row 3 K1, *k1, yo, k1, [p3, k1] 5 times, yo; rep from *, end last rep k2.

Row 4 P1, *p3, [k3, p1] 5 times, p1; rep from *, end last rep p3.

Row 5 K1, *[k1, yo] twice, [ssk, p2] 5 times, [k1, yo] twice; rep from *, end last rep k2.

Row 6 P2, *p4, [k2, p1] 5 times, p4; rep from *, end last rep p5.

Row 7 K1, *[k1, yo] 4 times, [ssk, p1] 5 times, [k1, yo] 4 times; rep from *, end last rep k2.

Row 8 P2, *p8, [k1, p1] 5 times, p8; rep from *, end last rep p9.

Row 9 K1, *k8, ssk 5 times, k8; rep from *, end last rep k10.

Row 10 P2, *p8, p4 and sl to cn, wrap yarn clockwise around sts on cn 3 times, sl to RH needle, p9; rep from *, end last rep p10.

Row 11 K1, *k8, p1, k4, p1, k7; rep from *, end last rep k9.

Row 12 K the knit sts and p the purl sts.

Row 13 K1, *k8, p1, sl 2 sts to cn and hold to back, k2, k2 from cn, p1, k7; rep from *, end last rep k9.

Row 14 Rep row 12.

Rep rows 11 to 14 until desired length, then cont as desired.

petite shells

▲ (beg as multiple of 5 sts plus 2 and end with multiple of 4 sts plus 1)

Row 1 (RS) K1, yo, *k5, sl the 2nd, 3rd, 4th and 5th st over the first st, yo; rep from *, end k1.

Row 2 P1, *[p1, yo, k1 tbl] in next st, p1; rep from * to end.

Row 3 K1, k1 tbl, *k3, k1 tbl; rep from *, end k3.

Rows 4, 5 and 6 Knit.

Cont as desired.

sea scallop edge

▲ (multiple of 11 sts)

Row 1 (RS) Knit.

Rows 2 and 4 Purl.

Row 3 *P2tog twice, [M1, k1] 3 times, M1, p2tog twice; rep from * to end.

Rows 5 and 6 Knit.

Row 7 *[K2, p2] twice, k1, p2; rep from * to end

Row 8 *K2, p1, [k2, p2] twice; rep from * to end.

Rep rows 7 and 8 for rib until desired length.

Cont as desired.

wrapped shell II

▲ (multiple of 10 sts plus 1)

• Sl all sts purlwise.

Row 1 (WS) P1, sl 2 wyif, *p5, sl 5 wyif; rep from * end last rep p5, sl 2 wyif, p1.

Row 2 K1, sl 2 wyib, *k5 and sl to cn, wrap yarn clockwise around these 5 sts 8 times, sl the 5 sts back to RH needle, sl 5 wyib; rep from *, end last rep sl 2 wyib, k1.

Row 3 P1, sl 2 wyif, *p4, insert RH needle purlwise into the next st and under the 2 strands from 2 rows below, p this st tog with the 2 strands, sl 5 wyif; rep from *, end last rep sl 2 wyif, p1.

Row 4 Purl, dec 1 st.

Work as foll in basketweave pat, rep rows 1 to 8 until desired length:

Rows 1 and 3 *K5, p5; rep from * to end.

Row 2 and all WS rows K the knit sts and p the purl sts.

Rows 5 and 7 *P5, k5; rep from * to end.

Row 8 Rep row 2.

Cont as desired.

picots

saw tooth lace

▶ Cast on 10 sts.

Row 1 Sl 1, k2, yo, k2tog, k1, yo twice, k2tog, yo twice, k2tog.

Row 2 Sl 1, k1, p1, k2, p1, k3, yo, k2tog, k1.

Row 3 Sl 1, k2, yo, k2tog, k3, yo twice, k2tog, yo twice, k2tog.

Row 4 Sl 1, k1, p1, k2, p1, k5, yo, k2tog, k1.

Row 5 Sl 1, k2, yo, k2tog, k5, yo twice, k2tog, yo twice, k2tog—16 sts.

Row 6 Sl 1, k1, p1, k2, p1, k7, yo, k2tog, k1.

Row 7 Sl 1, k2, yo, k2tog, k11.

Row 8 Bind off 6 sts, k6, yo, k2tog, k1—10 sts.

Rep rows 1 to 8 until desired length.

Bind off.

wrapped shell edge I

▲ (multiple of 8 sts plus 1)

• Sl all sts purlwise.

Row 1 (WS) With A, k1, sl 1 wyif ,*p5, sl 3 wyif; rep from *, end last rep sl 1 wyif, k1.

Row 2 With A, k1, sl 1 wyib, *k next 5 sts then sl these 5 sts to dpn and hold to front, then wind yarn from left to right (counter clockwise) evenly around the 5 sts on dpn 8 times, pass 5 sts from dpn back to RH needle, sl 3 wyib; rep from *, end last rep sl 1 wyib, k1.

Row 3 With A, k1, sl 1 wyif, *p4, insert RH needle purlwise into the next st and under the 2 strands from 2 rows below, p this st tog with the 2 strands, sl 3 wyif; rep from *, end last rep sl 1, k1.

Row 4 With A, purl.

Row 5 Change to B and purl.

Row 6 (RS) P2, *k5, p3; rep from *, end last rep p2.

Row 7 K the knit sts and p the purl sts.

Rep rows 6 and 7 for k5, p3 rib until desired length.

Cont as desired.

saw-tooth points with bobbles

▶ Make bobble (MB)

[K1, p1] twice, k1 in same st—5 sts, [turn, sl 1, k4] 4 times, turn, lift 4th, 3rd, and then 2nd st over first st.

Cast on 6 sts.

Row 1 (RS) K3, yo, k3.

Row 2 and all WS rows Knit.

Row 3 K3, yo, k4.

Row 5 K3, yo, k5.

Row 7 K3, yo, k6.

Row 9 K3, yo, k7.

Row 11 K3, yo, k7, MB—12 sts.

Row 12 Bind off 6 sts, k to end—6 sts.

Rep rows 1 to 12 until desired length. Bind off.

horizontal double bobble

▲ (multiple of 4 sts plus 1)

Make bobble (MB)

[K1, p1] twice, k1 in same st—5 sts, turn, k5, turn, p5, turn, k5, turn, sl 2nd, 3rd, 4th and 5th st over first st, turn, k1.

Rows 1 and 2 Knit.

Rows 3 and 7 (RS) K2, *MB, k3; rep from *, end last rep MB, k2.

Rows 4 and 6 K2, p to last 2 sts, k2.

Row 5 Knit.

Row 8 Rep row 4.

Cont as desired.

sugar scallops I

▲ (beg as a multiple of 11 sts plus 2 and end as a multiple of 6 sts plus 2)

Row 1 (WS) Purl.

Row 2 K2, *k1 and sl back to LH needle, with RH needle, lift next 8 sts, 1 at a time, over this st and off needle, yo twice, k the first st again, k2; rep from * to end.

Row 3 K1, *p2tog, drop first yo of previous row, k1, p1, k1 and p1 in second yo—4 sts, p1; rep from *, end k1.

Work 5 rows of garter stitch.

Cont as desired.

sugar scallops II

▲ Work rows 1 to 3 as for Sugar Scallops I.

Cont as desired.

sugar scallops III

▲ (beg as a multiple of 11 sts plus 2 and end as a multiple of 7 sts plus 2)

Rows 1 and 2 Work as for Sugar Scallops I.

Row 3 K1, *p2tog, drop first yo of previous row, k into front, back, front, back and front again in second yo—5 sts, p1; rep from *, end k1.

Cont in St st or as desired.

picots

garter stitch T twist

▲ (multiple of 6 sts)

K 10 rows.

Next row (RS) K6, then rotate the LH needle counter-clock-wise 360 degrees, then k another 6 sts and rotate the LH needle again counter-clockwise 360 degrees. Cont to k6 sts and rotate LH needle, to the end of the row.

Cont in garter st or as desired.

stockinette stitch T twist

▲ (multiple of 6 sts)

Work 6 rows in St st.

Next row (RS) K6, then rotate the LH needle counter-clock-wise 360 degrees, then k another 6 sts and rotate the LH needle again counter-clockwise 360 degrees. Cont to k6 sts and rotate LH needle, to the end of the row.

Cont in St st or as desired.

seed stitch T twist

▲ (multiple of 6 sts)

Work 6 rows in seed st.

Next row (RS) Work 6 sts in seed st, then rotate the LH needle counter-clockwise 360 degrees, then work another 6 sts in seed st and rotate the LH needle again counter-clockwise 360 degrees. Cont to work 6 sts and rotate LH needle, to the end of the row.

Cont in seed st or as desired.

points &

arrow bobble points

▲ (beg as a multiple of 13 sts plus 2 and end as a multiple of 10 sts plus 3)

Row 1 K1, *k2, SKP, [sl 2 sts tog, k3tog, p2sso], k2tog, k2; rep from *, end k1.

Row 2 P4, *yo, p1, yo, p6; rep from *, end last rep p4.

Row 3 K1, yo, *k2, SKP, k1, k2tog, k2, yo; rep from *, end k1.

Row 4 P2, *yo, p2, yo, p3, yo, p2, yo, p1; rep from *, end p1.

Row 5 K2, *yo, k1, yo, SKP, k1, SK2P, k1, k2tog, yo, k1, yo, k1; rep from *, end k1.

Row 6 Purl.

Row 7 K5, *yo, [sl 2 sts tog, k3tog, p2sso], yo, k7; rep from *, end last rep k5.

K 3 rows.

Make bobbles and sew to each point.

Cont as desired.

puff point bobbles

▲ (multiple of 10 sts plus 1)

Make Bobble (MB)

[K1, p1] twice in same st—4 sts, [turn, k4] 3 times, turn, lift 2nd, 3rd, and 4th st over first st, turn, k1.

Row 1 (RS) With A, *p5, MB, p4; rep from *, end last rep p5.

Row 2 and all WS rows Purl.

Row 3 *P1, yo, p2, ssp, k1, p2tog, p2, yo; rep from *, end p1.

Row 5 *P2, yo, p1, ssp, k1, p2tog, p1, yo, p1; rep from *, end last rep p2.

Row 7 *P3, yo, ssp, k1, p2tog, yo, p2; rep from *, end last rep p3.

Row 9 P5, *k1, p9; rep from *, end last rep p5.

Change to B and p 2 rows.

Change to C and p 2 rows.

Cont as desired.

festive mimosa

▲ (multiple of 24 sts plus 3)

Make bobble (MB)

[K1, p1] twice, in same st—4 sts, [turn, k4] 4 times, turn, with RH needle, lift 2nd, 3rd and 4th st over first st.

Rows 1 and 3 (RS) With CC, purl.

Row 2 Knit.

Row 4 Change to MC and purl.

Row 5 K1, k2tog, *[k1, yo] twice, k7, [sl 2 sts tog knitwise, k1, p2sso], k7, [yo, k1] twice, [sl 2 sts tog knitwise, k1, p2sso]; rep from *, end last rep ssk, k1.

Row 6 and all WS rows Purl.

Row 7 K1, k2tog, *k1, [k1, yo] twice, k2, MB, k3, [sl 2 sts tog knitwise, k1, p2sso], k3, MB, k2, [yo, k1] twice, k1, [sl 2 sts tog knitwise, k1, p2sso]; rep from *, end last rep ssk, k1.

Row 9 K1, k2tog, *MB, k1, [k1, yo] twice, k2, MB, k2, [sl 2 sts tog knitwise, k1, p2sso], k2, MB, k2, [yo, k1] twice, k1, MB, [sl 2 sts tog knitwise, k1, p2sso]; rep from *, end last rep ssk, k1.

Row 11 K1, k2tog, *k1, MB, k1, [k1, yo] twice, k2, MB, k1, [sl 2 sts tog knitwise, k1, p2sso], k1, MB, k2, [yo, k1] twice, k1, MB, k1, [sl 2 sts tog knitwise, k1, p2sso]; rep from *, end last rep ssk, k1.

Row 13 K1, k2tog, *k2, MB, k1, [k1, yo] twice, k2, MB, [sl 2 sts tog knitwise, k1, p2sso], MB, k2, [yo, k1] twice, k1, MB, k2, [sl 2 sts tog knitwise, k1, p2sso]; rep from *, end last rep ssk, k1.

Row 15 K1, k2tog, *k3, MB, k1, [k1, yo] twice, k2, [sl 2 sts tog knitwise, k1, p2sso], k2, [yo, k1] twice, k1, MB, k3, [sl 2 sts tog knitwise, k1, p2sso]; rep from *, end last rep ssk, k1.

Rows 17 With MC, knit.

Rows 18 and 20 With CC, knit.

Row 19 With CC, purl.

Cont as desired.

picots

eyelet points/bobbles

▲ (beg with 4 sts and end with multi-ple of 24 sts)

• Each point is worked separately, then all points are joined on the same row. Break yarn on all but last point and leave sts on needle.

Cast on 4 sts.

Row 1 Knit.

Row 2 and all WS rows Purl.

Row 3 [Yo, k1] 4 times.

Row 5 [Yo, k3, yo, k1] twice.

Row 7 [Yo, k5, yo, k1] twice.

Row 9 [Yo, k7, yo, k1] twice.

Row 11 [Yo, k9, yo, k1] twice—24 sts.

Row 12 Purl.

Row 13 Knit across, joining all points.

Make bobbles and sew to each point.

Cont as desired.

dew drops

▲ (Beg with 1 st and end with a multi-ple of 2 sts plus 1)

• Each point is worked separately, then all points are joined on the same row. Break yarn on all but last point and leave sts on needle.

Cast on 1 st. Work **3-Bobble Cluster** (see page 164).

Row 1 (RS) K1, p1, k1 in rem st of bob-ble—3 sts.

Row 2 and all WS rows Purl.

Row 3 K1, [yo, k1] twice.

Row 5 K2, yo, k1, yo, k2.

Row 7 K3, yo, k1, yo, k3.

Row 9 K4, yo, k1, yo, k4.

Row 11 K5, yo, k1, yo, k5—13 sts.

Row 12 Purl.

Break yarn and leave sts on needle.

On same needle, cast on and work rows 1 to 12 to make another point.

Cont in this manner until desired number of points are made.

Turn and p next row, joining all points then work as foll:

Rows 13, 15, 17 and 19 K1, *sl 1 wyif, k1; rep from * to end.

Rows 14, 16 and 18 P2, *sl 1 wyib, p1; rep from *, end last rep p2.

Cont as desired.

sugar drops

▲ (multiple of 13 sts)

• Each point is worked separately, then all points are joined on the same row. Break yarn on all but last point and leave sts on needle.

Cast on 1 st. Work **3-Bobble Cluster** (see page 164).

Row 1 (RS) [K1, yo, k1] in rem st of bobble.

Row 2 and all WS rows Purl.

Row 3 K1, [yo, k1] twice.

Row 5 K1, yo, k3, yo, k1.

Row 7 K1, yo, k5, yo, k1.

Row 9 K1, yo, k7, yo, k1.

Row 11 K1, yo, k9, yo, k1—13 sts.

Break yarn and leave sts on needle.

On same needle, cast on and work rows 1 to 11 to make another point.

Cont in this manner until desired number of points are made.

Turn and work across all points on needle to join and work as foll:

Rows 12 and 14 (WS) Purl.

Row 13 Knit.

Rows 15 and 18 *K1, p1; rep from *, end k1.

Rows 16 and 17 *P1, k1; rep from *, end p1.

Cont as desired.

multi point /overlay

▲ (multiple of 10 sts)

• Each point is worked separately, then all points are joined on the same row.
Break yarn after each point and leave sts on needle.
With MC, work in garter st for 1"/2.5cm. Bind off.
With A, work rows 1 to 9 of **Basic Horizontal Points** (see page 157)—10 sts,
alternating colors (B, C and A) until each point is 10 sts wide. Break yarn after
each color. With MC, work across all points to join.
Bind off. Sew points to garter-st background along bound-off edge.
With MC, pick up along bound-off edge and cont as desired.

stripe points

▲ (multiple of 10 sts)

• Each point is worked separately, then all points are joined on the same row.
Do not break yarns but leave sts on needle.
• When changing colors, twist yarn on WS to prevent holes.
Alternating colors as desired, work rows 1 to 9 of **Basic Horizontal Points** (see
page 157)—10 sts. Do not break yarn.
Work 14 rows in garter st across all points, working colors as established.
Cont as desired.

solid points with cord/bobbles

▲ (multiple of 10 sts)

• Each point is worked separately, then all points are joined on the same row. Break
yarn on all but last point and leave sts on needle.
Work rows 1 to 9 of **Basic Horizontal Points** (see page 157)—10 sts.
Cont across all sts and work in garter st until desired length.
With CC, work **I-cord** (see page 118) and **Bobbles** (see page 164).
Sew cord to RS along lower edge of points.
Make **Bobbles** and sew to center of each point.
Cont as desired.

picots

basic horizontal points/bobbles

▲ (multiple of 11 sts)

• Each point is worked separately, then all points are joined on the same row. Break yarn on all but last point and leave sts on needle.

Cast on 2 sts.

Row 1 K2.

Rows 2 to 10 Yo, k to end—11 sts.

Break yarn and leave sts on needle.

On same needle, cast on and work rows 1 to 10 to make another point. Cont in this manner until desired number of points are made. Turn and work across all points on needle to join.

Make **Bobbles** (see page 164) and sew to each point.

Cont as desired.

horizontal garter stitch scallops

▲ (multiple of 12 sts)

• Each point is worked separately, then all points are joined on the same row. Break yarn on all but last point and leave sts on needle.

Cast on 6 sts.

Row 1 K6.

Rows 2 to 6 Inc 1, k to end—11 sts.

Break yarn and leave sts on needle.

On same needle, cast on and work rows 1 to 6 to make another point. Cont in this manner until desired number of points are made. Turn and work across all points on needle to join.

Cont as desired.

vertical garter stitch scallops

▶ Cast on 7 sts. K 1 row. ◀◀

Row 1 K5, inc 1, k1.

Row 2 K1, inc 1, k6.

Row 3 K7, inc 1, k1.

Row 4 K1, inc 1, k8.

Row 5 K9, inc 1, k1.

Row 6 K1, inc 1, k10.

Row 7 K11, inc 1, k1.

Row 8 K1, inc 1, k12—15 sts.

Row 9 K12, k2tog, k1.

Row 10 K1, k2tog, k11.

Row 11 K10, k2tog, k1.

Row 12 K1, k2tog, k9.

Row 13 K8, k2tog, k1.

Row 14 K1, k2tog, k7.

Row 15 K6, k2tog, k1.

Row 16 K1, k2tog, k5—7 sts.

Rep rows 1 to 16 until desired length.

Bind off.

wave diamond border

▶ Cast on 16 sts.

K 1 row.

Row 1 Sl 1, k1, yo, k2tog, k8, k2tog, yo, k2.

Row 2 Yo, k16.

Row 3 Sl 1, k1, yo, k2tog, k7, k2tog, yo, k4.

Row 4 Yo, k17.

Row 5 Sl 1, k1, yo, k2tog, k6, k2tog, yo, k6.

Row 6 Yo, k18.

Row 7 Sl 1, k1, yo, k2tog, k5, k2tog, yo, k8.

Row 8 Yo, k19.

Row 9 Sl 1, k1, yo, k2tog, k4, k2tog, yo, k10.

Row 10 Yo, k20.

Row 11 Sl 1, k1, yo, k2tog, k3, k2tog, yo, k12.

Row 12 Yo, k21.

Row 13 Sl 1, k1, yo, k2tog, k2, k2tog, yo, k14.

Row 14 Yo, k22.

Row 15 Sl 1, k1, yo, k2tog, k1, k2tog, yo, k16.

Row 16 Yo, k2tog, k21.

Row 17 Sl 1, k1, yo, k2tog, k3, yo, k2tog, k14.

Row 18 Yo, k2tog twice, k19.

Row 19 Sl 1, k1, yo, k2tog, k4, yo, k2tog, k12.

Row 20 Yo, k2tog twice, k18.

Row 21 Sl 1, k1, yo, k2tog, k5, yo, k2tog, k10.

Row 22 Yo, k2tog twice, k17.

Row 23 Sl 1, k1, yo, k2tog, k6, yo, k2tog, k8.

Row 24 Yo, k2tog twice, k16.

Row 25 Sl 1, k1, yo, k2tog, k7, yo, k2tog, k6.

Row 26 Yo, k2tog twice, k15.

Row 27 Sl 1, k1, yo, k2tog, k8, yo, k2tog, k4.

Row 28 Yo, k2tog twice, k14.

Row 29 Sl 1, k1, yo, k2tog, k9, yo, k2tog, k2.

Row 30 Yo, k2tog twice, K 13—16 sts.

Rep rows 1 to 30 until desired length.

Bind off.

french waves

▶ Cast on 23 sts.

• Sl all sts purlwise.

Row 1 Sl 1, k2, [yo, k2tog] twice, k1, yo, k1, [yo, k2tog] 7 times.

Row 2 K18, [yo, k2tog] twice, k2.

Row 3 Sl 1, k2, [yo, k2tog] twice, k1, yo, k16.

Row 4 K19, [yo, k2tog] twice, k2.

Row 5 Sl 1, k2, [yo, k2tog] twice, k1, yo, k17.

Row 6 K20, [yo, k2tog] twice, k2.

Row 7 Sl 1, k2, [yo, k2tog] twice, k1, yo, k18.

Row 8 K21, [yo, k2tog] twice, k2.

Row 9 Sl 1, k2, [yo, k2tog] twice, k1, yo, k19.

Row 10 K22, [yo, k2tog] twice, k2.

Row 11 Sl 1, k2, [yo, k2tog] twice, k1, yo, k20.

Row 12 Bind off 5 sts, [yo, k2tog] 7 times, k3, [yo, k2tog] twice, k2.

Rep rows 3 to 12 until desired length, end with row 11. Bind off.

purl scallop

▼ Work in St st for 1½"/4cm.

Then work in rev St st for 3"/7.5cm or twice the width of desired border. Break yarn, leaving a long end for sewing.

Next row Fold border in half, WS tog.

On WS of work, sew sts off needle, one at a time, attaching each st to corresponding st at beg of border. Every 10th st, pass sewing yarn around and over top of border and pull tight to form scallop.

picots

angel wings scallop edging

▶ Cast on 12 sts.

K 1 row.

Row 1 Sl 1, k2, [yo, k2tog] twice, k2, yo, k1, yo, k2.

Row 2 Sl 1, k1, p3, k3, [yo, k2tog] twice, k2.

Row 3 Sl 1, k2, [yo, k2tog] twice, k7.

Row 4 Rep row 2.

Row 5 Sl 1, k2, [yo, k2tog] twice k2, [yo, k1] 3 times, yo, k2.

Row 6 Sl 1, k1, p7, k3, [yo, k2tog] twice, k2.

Row 7 Sl 1, k2, [yo, k2tog] twice, k11.

Row 8 Rep row 6.

Row 9 Sl 1, k2, [yo, k2tog] twice, k2, [yo, k1] 7 times, yo, k2.

Row 10 Sl 1, k1, p15, k3, [yo, k2tog] twice, k2.

Row 11 Sl 1, k2, [yo, k2tog] twice, k19.

Row 12 Rep row 10.

Row 13 Sl 1, k2, [yo, k2tog] twice, k2, [yo, k1] 15 times, yo, k2.

Row 14 Sl 1, k1, p31, k3, [yo, k2tog] twice, k2.

Row 15 Sl 1, k2, [yo, k2tog] twice, k35.

Row 16 Bind off 30 sts, p2, k3, [yo, k2tog] twice, k2.

Rep rows 1 to 14.

Next row Sl 1, k2, [yo, k2tog] twice, k34, sl last st, pick up and k 9th st of previous scallop, pass sl st over it.

Next row Rep row 16.

Rep these last 16 rows until desired length.

Bind off.

joanie's jubilee

▶ Cast on 22 sts.

Row 1 (RS) Sl 1, k1, yo, k2tog, [p2, k2] 3 times, p1, M1, work 5 sts in seed st.

Rows 2 and 18 Work 6 sts in seed st, k1, [p2, k2] 3 times, k1, yo, k2tog, k1.

Row 3 Sl 1, k1, yo, k2tog, [p2, k2] 3 times, p1, M1, work 6 sts in seed st.

Rows 4 and 16 Work 7 sts in seed st, k1, [p2, k2] 3 times, k1, yo, k2tog, k1.

Row 5 Sl 1, k1, yo, k2tog, [p2, k2] 3 times, p1, M1, work 7 sts in seed st.

Rows 6 and 14 Work 8 sts in seed st, k1, [p2, k2] 3 times, k1, yo, k2tog, k1.

Row 7 Sl 1, k1, yo, k2tog, [p2, k2] 3 times, p1, M1, work 8 sts in seed st.

Rows 8 and 12 Work 9 sts in seed st, k1, [p2, k2] 3 times, k1, yo, k2tog, k1.

Row 9 Sl 1, k1, yo, k2tog, [p2, k2] 3 times, p1, M1, work 9 sts in seed st—27 sts.

Row 10 Work 10 sts in seed st, k1, wyif wrap yarn clockwise around rem 16 sts on LH needle 3 times, then [p2, k2] 3 times, k1, yo, k2tog, k1.

Row 11 Sl 1, k1, yo, k2tog, [p2, k2] 3 times, p1, k2tog, work 8 sts in seed st.

Row 13 Sl 1, k1, yo, k2tog, [p2, k2] 3 times, p1, k2tog, work 7 sts in seed st.

Row 15 Sl 1, k1, yo, k2tog, [p2, k2] 3 times, p1, k2tog, work 6 sts in seed st.

Row 17 Sl 1, k1, yo, k2tog, [p2, k2] 3 times, p1, k2tog, work 5 sts in seed st.

Row 19 Sl 1, k1, yo, k2tog, [p2, k2] 3 times, p1, k2tog, work 4 sts in seed st—22 sts.

Row 20 Work 5 sts in seed st, k1, [p2, k2] 3 times, k1, yo, k2tog, k1.

Rep rows 1 to 20 until desired length.

Bind off.

patterns

TUTTI TWIST CARDIGAN

SIZES

To fit Small (Medium, Large). Directions are for smallest size with larger sizes in parentheses. If there is only one figure, it applies to all sizes.

KNITTED MEASUREMENTS:

- Bust (buttoned) 39½ (46, 52)"/100 (117, 132)cm
- Length 28"/71cm
- Upper arm 14 (15, 16½)"/35.5 (38, 42)cm

MATERIALS

- 16 (18, 20) 1¾oz/50g balls (each approx 98yd/90m) of Karabella Yarns *Aurora 8* (wool) in #16 rust (4)
- Size 8 (5mm) circular needles, 29"/74cm long
- Cable needle
- Stitch holders and markers
- Seven ⅞"/22mm buttons

GAUGE

18 sts and 26 rows = 4"/10cm over St st using size 8 (5mm) needles.
TAKE TIME TO CHECK GAUGE.

Note: Body of cardigan is worked in one piece to the underarm.

Tutti Twists

(multiple of 14 sts)
Rows 1 and 2 Knit.
Row 3 (WS) *[P1, k2] twice, p2, [k2, p1] twice; rep from * to end.
Row 4 *[1/1 LPC, p1] twice, k2, [p1, 1/1 RPC] twice; rep from * to end.
Rows 5 and 19 *K1, p1, k2, p1, k1, p2, k1, p1, k2, p1, k1; rep from * to end.
Row 6 *[P1, 1/1 LPC] twice, k2, [1/1 RPC, p1] twice; rep from * to end.
Rows 7 and 17 *K2, p1, k2, p4, k2, p1, k2; rep from * to end.
Row 8 *P2, 1/1 LPC, p1, k4, p1, 1/1 RPC, p2; rep from * to end.
Rows 9 and 15 *K3, p1, k1, p4, k1, p1, k3; rep from * to end.
Row 10 *P3, 1/1 LPC, k4, 1/1 RPC, p3; rep from * to end.
Rows 11 and 13 *K4, p6, k4; rep from * to end.
Row 12 *P4, 6-st RC, p4; rep from * to end.
Row 14 *P3, 1/1 RPC, k4, 1/1 LPC, p3; rep from * to end.
Row 16 *P2, 1/1 RPC, p1, k4, p1, 1/1 LPC, p2; rep from * to end.
Row 18 *[P1, 1/1 RPC] twice, k2, [1/1 LPC, p1] twice; rep from * to end.
Row 20 *[1/1 RPC, p1] twice, k2, [p1, 1/1 LPC] twice; rep from * to end.
Row 21 (WS) Rep row 3.
Row 22 to 24 Knit.
Rep rows 1 to 24 for Tutti Twists.

BODY

Cast on 206 (234, 262) sts.
Row 1 (WS) P5, pm, work row 1 of Tutti Twists pat to last 5 sts, pm, p5.
Note On foll rows, sl markers every row. Always slip sts with yarn in back on RS rows.
Row 2 K4, sl 1, work pat row 2 to next marker, sl 1, k4.
Rows 3 to 19 Work in pats as established.
Row 20 (Buttonhole row) K4, sl 1, [1/1RPC, p1] twice, yo, k2tog, [p1, 1/1LPC] twice, work to next marker, sl 1, k4.
Row 21 Work pats as established, working p1 into yo.

Rows 22 and 24 K4, sl 1, k to next marker, sl 1, k4.
Row 23 P5, k to next marker, p5.
Note Pat rows 1 and 2 will NOT be worked on the next 2 rows only.

Front borders and body

Next row (WS) P5, work pat row 3 over next 14 sts, k1 (garter st border), pm, p to last 20 sts, pm, k1 (garter st border), work pat row 3 over next 14 sts, p5.

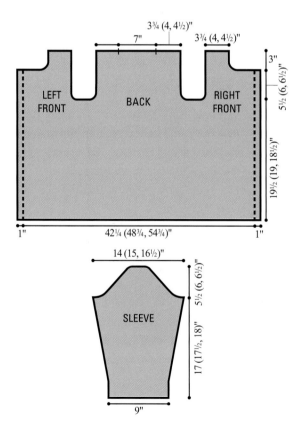

Next row K4, sl 1, work pat row 4 over 14 sts, k1, k to next marker, k1, work pat row 4 over 14 sts, sl 1, k4.
Cont in pats as established, beg with pat row 5 and work six more buttonholes on every pat row 20 as before.
Note The first and last 5 sts are facing sts that will be folded to the WS at finishing and there is 1 garter st separating the Tutti Twists pat and St st of the body. Work Tutti Twist pat through row 24, then cont to rep rows 1 to 24.
Work until piece measures 19½ (19, 18½)"/49.5 (48, 47)cm from beg, end with a WS row.

Divide for back and fronts

Next row (RS) Work 52 (58, 64) sts and place on a holder, bind off next 12 (14, 16) sts for underarm, k until there are 78 (90, 102) sts on RH needle for back, bind off next 12 (14, 16) sts, work to end and place these last 52 (58, 64) sts on a 2nd holder. Cut yarn.

Back

Rejoin yarn to center back sts and p 1 row on WS. Work on back sts only in St st, and cont armhole shaping as foll: bind off 3 sts at beg of next 0 (2, 4) rows, 2 sts at beg of next 0 (2, 4) rows, dec 1 st each side every other row 6 (6, 5) times—66 (68, 72) sts. Work even until armhole measures 8½ (9, 9½)"/21.5 (23, 24)cm. Bind off all sts.

Right front

Sl 52 (58, 64) sts from right front holder to needle. Join yarn at underarm edge and work in pats, working armhole shaping at underarm edge only same as back—46 (47, 49) sts. Work even until armhole measures approx 5½ (6, 6½)"/14 (15.5, 16.5)cm, end with a pat row 23.

Neck shaping

Next row (RS) Bind off 20 sts (neck edge), work to end. Cont to bind off 2 sts from neck edge twice, dec 1 st every other row 5 times—17 (18, 20) sts. Work even until same length as back. Bind off sts for shoulder.

Left front

Slip left front sts from holder to needle. Complete to correspond to right front, reversing all shaping.

SLEEVES

Cast on 44 sts.

Row 1 (WS) P1, work row 1 of Tutti Twists pat over 42 sts, p1.

Cont in pats as established, working first and last st in St st, through row 23, inc 0 (0, 2) sts on last row—44 (44, 46) sts.

Cont in St st over all sts, inc 1 st each side on row 7, then every 6th row 0 (6, 13) times, every 8th row 9 (5, 0) times—64 (68, 74) sts. Work even until piece measures 17 (17½, 18)"/43 (44.5, 45.5)cm from beg.

Cap shaping

Bind off 6 (7, 8) sts at beg of next 2 rows. Dec 1 st each side every RS row 14 (15, 17) times. Bind off 2 sts at beg of next 6 rows. Bind off rem 12 sts.

COLLAR

Cast on 116 sts.

Row 1 K2, work row 1 of Tutti Twists pat over 112 sts, k2. Cont in pats as established, working first and last 2 sts in garter st, until pat row 23 has been worked.

Beg rib

Row 1 (RS) K2, *k1, p2, k1, p2, k2, p2, k1, p2, k1; rep from *, end k2.

Row 2 K2, *p1, k2, p1, k2, p2, k2, p1, k2, p1; rep from *, end k2.

Rep rows 1 and 2 for 2"/5cm. Leave sts on needle.

FINISHING

Beg at center of right front band, pick up 116 sts around neck to center of left front band. Hold RS of collar to WS of neck, use 3 needle bind-off to attach collar to neck as foll: With needles parallel, insert 3rd needle into first st on both needles and k them tog, work next st from each needle tog, pass the first st over the 2nd to bind off. Cont in this way until all sts are bound-off.

Fold facing at front edges to WS along slip st and sew in place.

Set in sleeves. Sew side sleeve seams. Weave in ends. Sew buttons to left front opposite buttonholes.

RUFFLES
LAYERED RUFFLE BAG

MATERIALS

- 3 1¾oz/50g skeins (each approx 143yd/130m) of Muench Yarns *Serpentine* (polyamide) in #906 blue (4)
- Three size 6 (4mm) needles or size to obtain gauge
- One set (2) size 5 (3.75mm) dpn
- Purse Frame #LV 61

GAUGE

26 sts and 36 rows = 4"/10 cm over St st using larger needles.
TAKE TIME TO CHECK GAUGE.

BAG BACK

*Cast on 49 sts for lower edge. Work in St st until piece measures 1½"/4cm from beg. Place sts on a spare needle.

Ruffle

Cast on 96 sts. K 2 rows.

Beg with WS row and work in St st until piece measures 1¾"/4.5cm from beg, end with a WS row.

Next (dec) row (RS) K1, k2tog across, k1—49 sts.

Join layers

Join, using the 3-needle joining technique.* Rep between *'s 3 times more—4 ruffles. Work in St st for 6 rows. K next row on WS for turning ridge, then work in St st for 6 rows more. Bind off.

FRONT

Work as for back.

FINISHING

Sew cast-on edge of front and back tog for bottom seam. Sew side seams to top of 3rd ruffle, sewing sides of ruffles tog, leaving 4th ruffle open.

Fold top at turning ridge over rod of purse frame and sew on WS.

Thread tapestry needle and wrapping yarn around side bar of frames, sew side opening edge of bag (NOT 4th ruffle) to frame.

I-cord handle

With dpn, cast on 3 sts. *Slide sts to beg of needle without turning and k3; rep from * until I-cord measures 16"/40.5cm. Thread I-cord halfway through ring at top of handle. Knot the I-cord 4"/10cm from ring. Thread open end through 2nd ring and sew I-cord closed.

LACE
VINTAGE LACE PULLOVER

SIZES

To fit Small (Medium, Large). Directions are for smallest size with larger sizes in parentheses. If there is only one figure, it applies to all sizes.

KNITTED MEASUREMENTS

- Bust 36 (40, 44)"/91.5 (101.5, 112)cm
- Length 23 (24, 25)"/58.5 (61, 63.5)cm
- Upper arm 13 (14, 15)"/33 (35.5, 38)cm

MATERIALS

- 8 (9, 10) 1¾oz/50g skeins (each approx 125yd/113m) of Classic Elite Yarn *Posh* (cashmere/silk) in #93052 pink (4)
- One pair size 7 (4.5mm) needles or size to obtain gauge
- Size 7 (4.5mm) circular needle, 16"/40cm long

GAUGE

19 sts and 26 rows = 4"/10cm over St st using size 7 (4.5mm) needles.
TAKE TIME TO CHECK GAUGE.

Border Pattern

Elizabeth's Lace Lattice

Note: This border is made vertically. It is worked separately and then sewn to a finished piece or sts may be picked up along the border to work the piece.

Cast on 23 sts.

K 1 row.

Row 1 (RS) Sl 1, k2, *yo, k2tog; rep from * to end.

Rows 2 and 4 K17, p1, k1, p1, k3.

Rows 3 and 5 Sl 1, k2, [yo, k2tog] twice, k16.

Row 6 K1, *yo 4 times, k1; rep from * to last 6 sts, p1, k1, p1, k3.

Row 7 Sl 1, k2, [yo, k2tog] twice, *drop the 4 yo's, sl next st; rep from * to end—16 long sts, then sl the 16 long sts back to LH needle then [sl sts 5 to 8 over sts 1 to 4 and back to LH needle, k8] twice.

Row 8 K17, p1, k1, p1, k3.

Row 9 Rep row 3.

Row 10 Rep row 2.

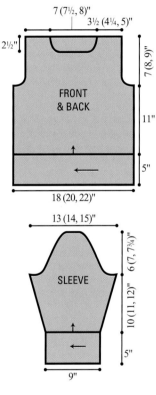

Rep rows 1 to 10 until desired length, end with row 2.
Bind off.

BACK

Cast on 23 sts. Rep rows 1 to 10 of border pat until piece measures approx 18 (20, 22)"/46 (51, 56)cm. Bind off.

With RS facing, pick up and k 86 (95, 105) sts evenly along side edge of border.

Work in St st until piece measures 11"/28cm above border, end with a WS row.

Armhole shaping

Bind off 5 sts at beg of next 2 rows, 3 sts at beg of next 2 rows, then dec 1 st each side every other row twice—66 (75, 85) sts. Work even until armhole measures 7 (8, 9)"/18 (20.5, 23)cm. Bind off.

FRONT

Work same as for back until armhole measures 4½ (5½, 6½)"/11.5 (14, 16.5)cm, end with a WS row.

Neck shaping

K23 (27, 31) sts, join a 2nd ball of yarn and bind off center 20 (21, 23) sts, work to end. Working both sides at once, bind off at each neck edge 3 sts once, 2 sts once, then dec 1 st each side every other row twice. Work even until piece measures same as back. Bind off rem 16 (20, 24) sts each side for shoulders.

SLEEVES

Cast on 23 sts. Rep rows 1 to 10 of border pat until piece measures approx 9"/23cm. Bind off.

With RS facing, pick up and k 43 sts evenly along side edge of border. Work in St st, inc 1 st each side every 4th row 0 (3, 6) times, every 6th row 9 (9, 8) times—61 (67, 71) sts. Work even until piece measures 10 (11, 12)"/25.5 (28, 30.5)cm above border.

Cap shaping

Bind off 4 sts at beg of next 2 rows, 2 sts at beg of next 2 rows, then dec 1 st each side every other row 16 (19, 21) times, bind off 2 sts at beg of next 4 rows. Bind off rem 9 sts.

FINISHING

Block pieces to measurements. Sew shoulder seams.

Neckband

With RS facing and circular needle, pick up and k 82 (84, 88) sts evenly around neck edge. Join and p 1 rnd, k 1 rnd, p 1 rnd.

Next (eyelet) rnd *Yo, k2tog; rep from * around. [P 1 rnd, k 1 rnd] twice. Bind off loosely purlwise. Set in sleeves. Beg above edging and sew sleeve seam, leaving edging open. Beg above edging and sew side seams, leaving edging open.

FRINGES
CORKSCREW FRINGE SCARF

KNITTED MEASUREMENTS

9½" x 36"/24cm x 91.5cm (without fringe)

MATERIALS

• 4 1¾oz/50g skeins (each approx 175yd/158m) of Koigu Wool Designs *Painter's Palette Premium Merino* (wool) in #621 red multi (**2**)

• Size 3 (3.25mm) needles or size to obtain gauge

GAUGE

26 sts and 36 rows = 4"/10cm over box st using size 3 (3.25mm) needles.
TAKE TIME TO CHECK GAUGE.

BOX STITCH

(multiple of 4 sts plus 2)

Rows 1 and 4 K2, *p2, k2; rep from * to end.
Rows 2 and 3 P2, *k2, p2; rep from * to end.
Rep rows 1 to 4 for box st.
Note Adjust yarn amounts accordingly if changing the length.

SCARF

Cast on 62 sts.
Work in box st until piece measures 36"/91.5cm from beg or desired length. Bind off.

FINISHING

Block piece to measurements.

Corkscrew Fringe

The fringe is knitted separately and then attached.
Loosely cast on 40 sts.
Row 1 [K1, k1 tbl, k1] in each st across.
Row 2 Bind off purlwise.
Finger twist each tassel into a corkscrew.
Make 22 corkscrews.
Attach 11 corkscrews evenly spaced across each end.

FLORA
BERRY CLUSTER PULLOVER

SIZES

To fit Small (Medium, Large). Directions are for smallest size with larger sizes in parentheses. If there is only one figure, it applies to all sizes.

KNITTED MEASURMENTS

• Bust 38 (42, 46)"/96.5 (106.5, 117)cm
• Length 20 (21, 22)"/51 (53.5, 56)cm
• Upper arm 13 (14, 15)"/33 (35.5, 38)cm

MATERIALS

• 9 (10, 12) .87oz/25g balls (each approx 108yd/100m) of Tahki Yarns/Tahki•Stacy Charles, Inc. *Jolie* (angora/wool) in #5016 mint (**4**)
• One pair size 7 (4.5mm) needles or size to obtain gauge
• Size 7 (4.5mm) circular needle, 16"/40cm long
• 1 package white pearls size 6mm
• Matching sewing thread

GAUGE

22 sts and 28 rows = 4"/10cm over St st using size 7 (4.5mm) needles.
TAKE TIME TO CHECK GAUGE.

Berry Cluster II with Beads

(multiple of 23 sts)

Row 1 (RS) *K8, k2tog, yo, k1, p1, k1, yo, ssk, k8; rep from * to end.
Row 2 *P7, p2tog tbl, p2, yo, k1, yo, p2, p2tog, p7; rep from * to end.
Row 3 *K6, k2tog, k1, yo, k2, p1, k2, yo, k1, ssk, k6; rep from * to end.
Row 4 *P5, p2tog tbl, p3, yo, p1, k1, p1, yo, p3, p2tog, p5; rep from * to end.
Row 5 *K4, k2tog, k2, yo, k3, p1, k3, yo, k2, ssk, k4; rep from * to end.
Row 6 *P3, p2tog tbl, p4, yo, p2, k1, p2, yo, p4, p2tog, p3; rep from * to end.
Row 7 *K2, k2tog, k3, yo, k4, p1, k4, yo, k3, ssk, k2; rep from * to end.
Row 8 *P1, p2tog tbl, p5, yo, p3, k1, p3, yo, p5, p2tog, p1; rep from * to end.
Row 9 *K2tog, k4, yo, k5, p1, k5, yo, k4, ssk; rep from * to end.
Row 10 *P11, k1, p11; rep from * to end.
Row 11 *K11, p1, k11; rep from * to end.
Row 12 Rep row 10.

BACK

Cast on 104 (115, 127) sts. K 2 rows.

Beg Berry Cluster pat

Row 1 K6 (0, 6), work pat over next 92 (115, 115) sts, k6 (0, 6). Cont in pat as established through row 12, then rep rows 1 to 12 once more. Work in St st until piece measures 13"/33cm from beg, end with a WS row.

Armhole shaping

Bind off 5 sts at beg of next 2 rows, 3 sts at beg of next 2 rows, 2 sts at beg on next 2 rows, then dec 1 st each side on next row—82 (93, 105) sts. Work even until armhole measures 7 (8, 9)"/18 (20.5, 23)cm. Bind off.

FRONT

Work as for back until armhole measures 4½ (5½, 6½)"/11.5 (14, 16.5)cm, end with a WS row.

Neck shaping

Next row (RS) K26 (30, 35), join a 2nd ball of yarn, bind off center 30 (33, 35) sts, work to end. Working both sides at once, bind off at each neck edge 3 sts once, 2 sts once, then dec 1 st every other row twice. Work even until piece measures same as back. Bind off rem 19 (23, 28) sts each side for shoulders.

SLEEVES

Cast on 46 sts. K 2 rows. Work rows 1 to 12 of Berry Cluster pat. Work in St st, inc 1 st each side every 4th row 0 (3, 8) times, every 6th row 13 (12, 10) times—72 (76, 82) sts. Work even until piece measures 15 (15½, 16)"/38 (39.5, 41)cm from beg.

Cap shaping

Bind off 5 sts at beg of next 2 rows, 2 sts at beg of next 4 rows, dec 1 st each side every

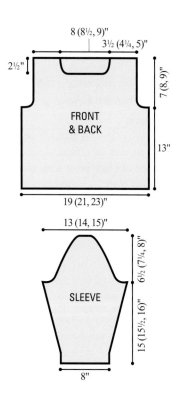

8 (8½, 9)"

3½ (4¼, 5)"

2½"

7 (8, 9)"

13"

FRONT & BACK

19 (21, 23)"

13 (14, 15)"

6½ (7¼, 8)"

SLEEVE

15 (15½, 16)"

8"

other row 18 (20, 23) times, bind off 2 sts at beg of next 4 rows. Bind off rem 10 sts.

FINISHING
Block pieces to measurements.
Using sewing thread, sew beads to clusters at lower edge of front, back and sleeves (foll photo.)
Sew shoulder seams. Set in sleeves. Sew side and sleeve seams.

Neckband
With RS facing and circular needle, pick up and k 84 (90, 94) sts evenly around neck edge. Join and work in rnds of St st for 1½"/4cm. P next row for turning ridge. Cont in St st for 1½"/4cm more. Bind off. Fold band to WS at turning ridge and sew to inside of neck edge.

POINTS & PICOTS
SUGAR DROPS

SIZES
To fit Small (Medium, Large). Directions are for smallest size with larger sizes in parentheses. If there is only one figure, it applies to all sizes.

KNITTED MEASUREMENTS
• Bust 38 (43, 48)"/96.5 (109, 122)cm
• Length 17 (18, 19)"/43 (46, 48)cm
• Upper arm 13 (14, 16)"/33 (35.5, 40.5)cm

MATERIALS
• 8 (9, 11) 1¾oz/50g skeins (each approx 103yd/95m) of Tahki Yarns/Tahki•Stacy Charles, Inc. *New Tweed* (wool/silk/cotton/viscose) in #02 maize (4)
• One pair size 8 (5mm) needles or size to obtain gauge

• Size 8 (5mm) circular needle, 16"/40cm long

GAUGE
19 sts and 24 rows = 4"/10cm over St st using size 8 (5mm) needles.
TAKE TIME TO CHECK GAUGE.

3-Bobble Cluster
Cast on 1 st.
Row 1 (RS) K1, p1, k1, p1 and k1 again in same st—5 sts.
Row 2 and all WS rows Sl 1, p4.
Rows 3, 5 and 7 Sl 1, k4.
Row 9 K2tog, k1, k2tog—3 sts.
Row 10 P3tog, turn.
Fold bobble in half, WS tog. Insert RH needle into cast-on st and k it tog with rem st of bobble—1 st.
Rep rows 1 to 10 twice more, leaving last st on needle.

SUGAR DROPS
• Each point is worked separately, then all points are joined on the same row. Break yarn on all but last point and leave sts on needle.
Cast on 1 st. Work 3-Bobble Cluster.
Row 1 (RS) [K1, yo, k1] in rem st of bobble.
Row 2 and all WS rows Purl.
Row 3 K1, [yo, k1] twice.
Row 5 K1, yo, k3, yo, k1.
Row 7 K1, yo, k5, yo, k1.
Row 9 K1, yo, k7, yo, k1.
Row 11 K1, yo, k9, yo, k1—13 sts.
Break yarn and leave sts on needle.
On same needle, cast on and work rows 1 to 11 to make another point.
Cont in this manner until all points are made.
Row 12 (WS) Turn and purl across all points on needle to join.
Row 13 Knit.
Row 14 Purl.
Rows 15 and 16 *K1, p1; rep from *, end k1.
Rows 17 and 18 *P1, k1; rep from *, end p1.

BACK
Work rows 1 to 11 of sugar drops 7 (8, 9) times—91 (104, 117) sts. Join points and dec 0 (dec 1, dec 1) st each side on next row—91

(102, 115) sts, then work rows 13 to 18 of sugar drops once, then rows 15 to 28 once more. Work in St st until piece measures 9"/23cm from beg (at start of point).

Armhole shaping
Bind off 5 sts at beg of next 2 rows, 3 sts at beg of next 2 rows, then dec 1 st each side every other row twice—71 (82, 95) sts. Work even until armhole measures 8 (9, 10)"/20.5 (23, 25.5)cm. Bind off.

FRONT
Work as for back until armhole measures 6 (7, 8)"/15 (18, 20.5)cm, end with a WS row.

Neck shaping
Next row (RS) K27 (32, 38) sts, join a 2nd ball of yarn and bind off center 17 (18, 19) sts, work to end. Working both sides at once, bind off at each neck edge 4 sts once, 3 sts once, 0 (0, 2) sts once, then dec 1 st each side every other row 1 (2, 1) times. Work even until same length as back. Bind off rem 19 (23, 28) sts each side for shoulders.

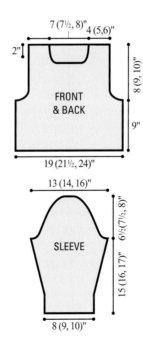

7 (7½, 8)"   4 (5,6)"
2"
FRONT & BACK
8 (9, 10)"
9"
19 (21½, 24)"

13 (14, 16)"
SLEEVE
6½(7½, 8)"
15 (16, 17)"
8 (9, 10)"

SLEEVES
Work rows 1 to 11 of sugar drops 3 (3, 4) times—39 (39, 52) sts. Join points and dec 1 (inc 4, dec 4) sts evenly spaced across next row—38 (43, 48) sts, then work rows (13 to 18). Work in St st, inc 1 st each side every 4th row 2 (0, 3) times, every 6h row 10 (12 11) times—62 (67, 76) sts. Work even until piece measures 15 (16, 17)"/38 (41, 43)cm from beg (at start of point).

Cap shaping
Bind off 5 sts at beg of next 2 rows, 2 sts at beg of next 2 rows, then dec 1 st each side every other row 16 (18, 20) times, bind off 2 (2, 3) sts at beg of next 4 rows—8 (9, 10) sts. Bind off.

FINISHING
Block pieces to measurements. Sew shoulder seams. Set in sleeves. Sew side and sleeve seams

Neckband
With RS facing and circular needle, pick up and k 80 (84, 88) sts evenly around neck edge. Join and work in rnds of k1, p1 rib for 1½"/4cm. Bind off loosely in rib.

FRINGES
SAXON BRAID SCARF

KNITTED MEASUREMENTS
5" x 50"/13cm x 127cm (without fringe)

MATERIALS
• 5 1¾oz/50g skeins (each approx 65yd/60m) of Classic Elite Yarns *Sinful* (cashmere) in #92026 blue (5)

• Size 10 (6mm) needles or size to obtain gauge
• Cable needle

GAUGE
14 sts and 20 rows = 4"/10cm over St st using size 10 (6mm) needles.
TAKE TIME TO CHECK GAUGE.

SAXON BRAID
Cast on 35 sts.
Rows 1 and 3 (WS) P1, k4, [p4, k4] 3 times, p1, p5.
Row 2 K5, k1 tbl, [p4, 4-st RC] 3 times, p4, k1 tbl.
Row 4 K5, k1 tbl, p3, 2/1 RPC, [2/2 LPC, 2/2 RPC] twice, 2/1 LPC, p3, k1 tbl.
Row 5 P1, k3, p2, k3, p4, k4, p4, k3, p2, k3, p1, p5.
Row 6 K5, k1 tbl, p3, 2/1 RPC, p2, 4-st LC, p4, 4-st LC, p3, 2/1 LPC, p2, k1 tbl.
Row 7 P1, k2, p2, [k4, p4] twice, k4, p2, k2, p1, p5.
Row 8 K5, k1 tbl, p2, k2, p2, [2/2 RPC, 2/1 LPC] twice, p2, k2, p2, k1 tbl.
Row 9 P1, [k2, p2] twice, k4, p4, k4, [p2, k2] twice, p1, p5.
Row 10 K5, k1 tbl, [p2, k2] twice, p4, 4-st RC, p4, [k2, p2] twice, k1 tbl.
Row 11 Rep row 9.
Row 12 K5, k1 tbl, p2, k2, p2, [2/2 LPC, 2/2 RPC] twice, p2, k2, p2, k1 tbl.
Row 13 P1, k2, p2, [k4, p4] twice, k4, p2, k2, p1, p5.
Row 14 K5, k1 tbl, p3, 2/1 RPC, p2, 4-st LC, p4, 4-st LC, p3, 2/1 LPC, p2, k1 tbl.
Row 15 P1, k3, p2, k3, p4, k4, p4, k3, p2, k3, p1, p5.
Row 16 K5, k1 tbl, p3, 2/1 LPC, [2/2 RPC, 2/2 LPC] twice, 2/1 RPC, p3, k1 tbl.

SCARF
Cast on 35 sts. Work rows 1 to 16 of saxon braid pat 16 times.
Bind off 29 sts and fasten off 30th st. Unravel last 5 sts and steam fringe lightly. Knot each fringe loop at scarf edge.

stitches

Inc 1
Knit into the front and back of next st.

Inc 2
[K1, p1, k1] in next st.

Inc 1 p-st
P1 into the front and back of next st.

M1 p-st
Lift the strand between last st worked and next st on the LH needle and purl it.

CDI (Central double increase)
[P1 tbl, p1] in next st, then insert LH needle into strand between the 2 sts just made and p it—3 sts.

K1B
Knit next st in the row below.

DD (Double decrease)
Sl 2 sts tog knitwise, k1, pass 2 sl sts over k st—2 sts dec.

SP2P
Sl 1 knitwise, p2tog, psso.

s2kp
Sl 2 sts tog, k1, pass the 2 sl sts over the k1—2 sts dec.

ssp
Sl 1, p1, psso.

Dec 4
P2tog, p3tog, pass the p2tog over the p3tog.

C3R
Sl 1 to cn and hold to *back*, p1, k1, k1 from cn.

SB1 (Slip bead)
Slip 1 bead as close as possible to LH needle.

ML (Make loop)
K1, wrapping yarn over needle, then wrap yarn over 1 or 2 fingers of left hand and then over needle again, draw both loops on needle through the st and place them on LH needle, k the 2 loops tog tbl.

Bobble I (smaller bobble)
K1, p1, k1 and p1 again all in next st—4 sts, turn, p4, turn, k4, turn, p2tog twice, turn and k2tog.

Bobble II (larger bobble)
Cast on 1 st. K in front, back, front, back and front again of st (5 sts made in one st).
Turn. Work 4 rows in St st.
With LH needle, lift 2nd, 3rd, 4th and 5th sts over first st—1 st.
Fasten off. Sew to piece.

MT (Make Tassel)
Insert needle into st knitwise, [wind yarn clockwise around 2 fingers and needle] 5 times, draw all 6 lps through the st and place them on the LH needle, then k them tog tbl.

3-needle joining technique
Work sts of both layers tog, using 3-needle joining technique as foll: with RS of layers facing (top layer over bottom layer) and the needles parallel, insert a third needle into the first st on each needle and work them tog.

3-Bobble Cluster
Cast on 1 st.
Row 1 RS [K1, p1] twice, k1 in same st—5 sts.
Row 2 and all WS rows Sl 1, p4.
Rows 3, 5 and 7 Sl 1, k4.
Row 9 K2tog, k1, k2tog—3 sts.
Row 10 P3tog, turn. Fold bobble in half, WS tog. Insert RH needle into cast-on st and k it tog with rem st of bobble—1 st.
Rep rows 1 to 10 twice more, leaving last st on needle.

RT
K2tog leaving sts on LH needle, then k first st again, sl both sts off needle.

LT
K the second st tbl, then k the first st and sl both sts off needle.

1/1 RPC
Sl 1 to cn and hold to *back*, k1, p1 from cn.

1/1 LPC
Sl 1 to cn and hold to *front*, p1, k1 from cn.

1/2 RC
Sl 1 to cn and hold to *back*, k2, k1 from cn.

1/2 LC
Sl 1 to cn and hold to *front*, k2, k1 from cn.

1/2 RPC
Sl 1 st to cn, hold in *back*, k2, p1 from cn.

1/3 RPC
Sl 1 to cn and hold to *back*, k3, p1 from cn.

2-st RC
Sl 1 to cn and hold to *back*, k1, k1 from cn.

2-st LC
Sl 1 to cn and hold to *front*, k1, k1 from cn.

2-st RPC
Sl 1 to cn and hold to *back*, p1, p1 from cn. Or p into *front* of second st, then p first st.

2-st LPC
Sl 1 to cn and hold to *front*, p1, p1 from cn.

2/1 RC
Sl 2 to cn and hold to *back*, k1, k2 from cn

2/1 LC
Sl 2 to cn and hold to *front*, k1, k2 from cn.

2/1 RPC
Sl 2 to cn and hold to *back*, k2, p1 from cn.

2/1 LPC
Sl 2 to cn and hold to *front*, p1, k2 from cn.

2/2 RPC
Sl 2 to cn and hold to *back*, k2, p2 from cn.

2/2 LPC
Sl 2 to cn and hold to *front*, p2, k2 from cn.

2/3 RPC
Sl 2 to cn and hold to *back*, k3, p2 from cn.

2/3 LPC
Sl 2 to cn and hold *front*, p3, k2 from cn.

3/1 LPC
Sl 3 to cn and hold to *front*, p1, k3 from cn.

3/1 RPC
Sl 1 and hold to *back*, k3, p1 from cn.

3/2 RPC
Sl 3 to cn and hold to *back*, k2, p3 from cn.

3/2 LPC
Sl 3 to cn and hold to *front*, p2, k3 from cn.

3/2 RTC
Sl 3 to cn, hold to *back*, k2, sl last st from cn back to LH needle and p1, then k2 from cn.

3/3 RPC
Sl 3 to cn and hold to *back*, k3, p3 from cn.

3/3 LPC
Sl 3 to cn and hold to *front*, p3, k3 from cn.

4-st RC
Sl 2 to cn and hold to *back*, k2, k2 from cn.

4-st LC
Sl 2 to cn and hold to *front*, k2, k2 from cn.

4/1 RPC
Sl 1 to cn and hold to *back*, k4, p1 from cn.

4/1 LPC
Sl 4 to cn and hold to *front*, p1, k4 from cn.

4-st RPC
Sl 2 to cn and hold to *back*, k2, p2 from cn.

5-st RPC
Sl 3 to cn and hold to *back*, k2, sl last st from cn to LH needle and p1, k2 from cn.

5-st LPC
Sl 2 to first cn and hold to *front*, sl 1 to second cn and hold to *back*, k2, p1 from second cn, k2 from first cn.

5-st RLC
Sl 1 to cn and hold to *front*, sl next 3 sts to 2nd cn and hold to *back*, k1, p3 from 2nd cn, k1 from first cn.

6-st RC
Sl 3 to cn and hold to *back*, k3, k3 from cn.

6-st LC
Sl 3 to cn and hold to *front*, k3, k3 from cn.

6-st RPC
Sl 3 sts to cn and hold to *back*, k3, p3 from cn.

7-st RC
Sl 3 sts to cn and hold to *back*, k4, k3 from cn.

7-st LC
Sl 4 to cn and hold to *front*, k3, k4 from cn.

abbreviations

approx approximately

beg begin(ning)

bind off Used to finish an edge and keep stitches from unraveling. Lift the first stitch over the second, the second over the third, etc. (UK: cast off)

cast on A foundation row of stitches placed on the needle in order to begin knitting.

CC contrast color

ch chain(s)

cm centimeter(s)

cn cable needle

cont continu(e)(ing)

dc double crochet (UK: tr-treble)

dec decrease(ing)—Reduce the stitches in a row (knit 2 together).

dpn double pointed needle(s)

foll follow(s)(ing)

g gram(s)

garter stitch Knit every row. Circular knitting: knit one round, then purl one round.

inc increase(ing)—Add stitches in a row (knit into the front and back of a stitch).

k knit

k2tog knit 2 stitches together

lp(s) loop(s)

LH left-hand

m meter(s)

MB make bobble (see "Stitches" page)

M1 make one stitch—With the needle tip, lift the strand between last stitch worked and next stitch on the left-hand needle and knit into the back of it. One stitch has been added.

MC main color

mm millimeter(s)

oz ounce(s)

p purl

psso pass slip stitch over

p2sso pass 2 slip stitches over

p2tog purl 2 stitches together

pat pattern

pick up and knit (purl) Knit (or purl) into the loops along an edge.

pm place marker—Place or attach a loop of contrast yarn or purchased stitch marker as indicated.

rem remain(s)(ing)

rep repeat

rev St st reverse Stockinette stitch—Purl right-side rows, knit wrong-side rows. Circular knitting: purl all rounds. (UK: reverse stocking stitch)

rnd(s) round(s)

RH right-hand

RS right side(s)

sc single crochet (UK: dc - double crochet)

sk skip

SKP Slip 1, knit 1, pass slip stitch over knit 1.

SK2P Slip 1, knit 2 together, pass slip stitch over k2tog.

sl slip—An unworked stitch made by passing a stitch from the left-hand to the right-hand needle as if to purl.

ssk slip, slip, knit—Slip next 2 stitches knitwise, one at a time, to right-hand needle. Insert tip of left-hand needle into fronts of these stitches from left to right. Knit them together. One stitch has been decreased.

st(s) stitch(es)

ssp slip, slip, purl—Work as for ssk, working purl instead of knit.

St st Stockinette stitch—Knit right-side rows, purl wrong-side rows. Circular knitting: knit all rounds. (UK: stocking stitch)

tbl through back of loop

tog together

WS wrong side(s)

w & t wrap and turn—Knit side–Wyib, sl next st purlwise. Move yarn between the needles to the front. Sl the same st back to LH needle. Turn work, bring yarn to the p side between needles. One st is wrapped. When working across the wrapped stitches, work to just before wrapped st, insert RH needle under the wrap and knitwise into the wrapped st, k them tog. **Purl side**–Wyif, sl next st purlwise. Move yarn between the needles to the back of work. Sl same st back to LH needle. Turn work, bring yarn back to the p side between the needles. One st is wrapped. When working across the wrapped stitches, work to just before wrapped st, insert RH needle from behind into the back lp of the wrap and place on LH needle; P wrap tog with st on needle.

wyif with yarn in front

wyib with yarn in back

work even Continue in pattern without increasing or decreasing. (UK: work straight)

yd yard(s)

yfrn Yarn forward and around needle—Used when making a yarn over after a knit stitch and before a purl stitch.

yo yarn over—Make a new stitch by wrapping the yarn over the right-hand needle. (UK: yfwd, yon, yrn)

* Repeat directions following * as many times as indicated.

[ ] Repeat directions inside brackets as many times as indicated.

t e c h n i q u e s

Pompom

1 Following the template, cut two circular pieces of cardboard.

2 Place tie strand between the circles. Wrap yarn around circles. Cut between circles

3 Knot tie strand tightly. Remove cardboard.

4 Place pompom between 2 smaller cardboard circles held together with a long needle and trim edges.

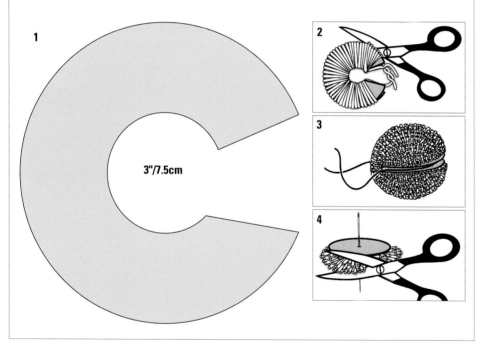

1

3"/7.5cm

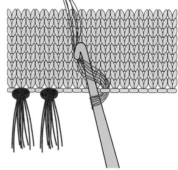

Lazy Daisy Stitch

Simple Fringe

Cut yarn twice desired length plus extra for knotting. On wrong side, insert hook from front to back through piece and over folded yarn. Pull yarn through. Draw ends through and tighten. Trim yarn.

Provisional Cast-On

Leaving tails about 4"/10cm long, tie a length of scrap yarn together with the main yarn in a knot. With your right hand, hold the knot on top of the needle a short distance from the tip, then place your thumb and index finger between the two yarns and hold the long ends with the other fingers. Hold your hand with your palm facing upwards and spread your thumb and index finger apart so that the yarn forms a "V" with the main yarn over your index finger and the scrap yarn over your thumb. Bring the needle up through the scrap yarn loop on your thumb from front to back. Place the needle over the main yarn on your index finger and then back through the loop on your thumb. Drop the loop off your thumb and placing your thumb back in the "V" configuration, tighten up the stitch on the needle. Repeat for the desired number of stitches. The main yarn will form the stitches on the needle and the scrap yarn will make the horizontal ridge at the base of the cast-on row.

When picking up the stitches along the cast-on edge, carefully cut and pull out the scrap yarn as you place the exposed loops on the needle. Take care to pick up the loops so that they are in the proper direction before you begin knitting.

acknowledgments

Special thanks to Chi Ling Moy for her artistic expertise and support. The Soho staff: Trisha Malcolm, Carla Scott, Michelle Lo and Art Joinnides for their commitment to excellence. I'd also like to extend my gratitude to Jack Deutsch and Eugene Mozgalevsky for the beautiful and detailed photography and to Nancy Henderson, Julie Sabella, Eileen Curry, Heris Stenzel and Charlotte Parry for the many hours devoted to helping me complete this major project. I am grateful to Classic Elite Yarns, Karabella Yarns, Koigu Wool Company, Muench Yarns and Diane Friedman and Stacy Charles of Tahki•Stacy Charles, Inc. for their generosity and support of this book.

Most importantly, I would also like to acknowledge my readers, students and all knitters and designers everywhere, who have been the inspiration for my "knitting on the edge" that keeps me on the path of creativity.

resources

Classic Elite Yarns
300A Jackson Street
Lowell, MA 01852

Filatura Di Crosa
distributed by
Tahki•Stacy Charles, Inc.

Muench Yarns, Inc.
285 Bel Marin Keys Blvd.
Unit J
Novato, CA 94949

Karabella Yarns, Inc.
1201 Broadway, Suite 311
New York, NY 10001

Koigu Wool Designs
RR #1
Williamsford, ON
NOH 2V0

Lacis
3163 Adeline St
Berkeley, CA 94703

Tahki Yarns
distributed by
Tahki•Stacy Charles, Inc.

Tahki•Stacy Charles, Inc.
8000 Cooper Ave.
Glendale, NY 11385